Adult Coloring Book Mandalas Design
45 Relax Design

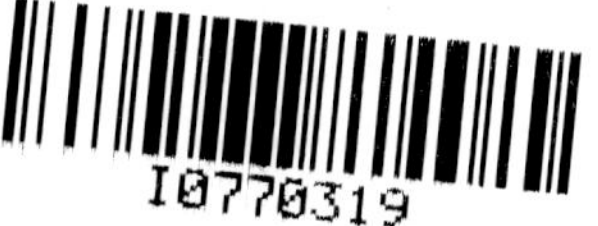

Adult Coloring Book Mandalas Design

ISBN-13: 978-1979065535

ISBN-10: 1979065535

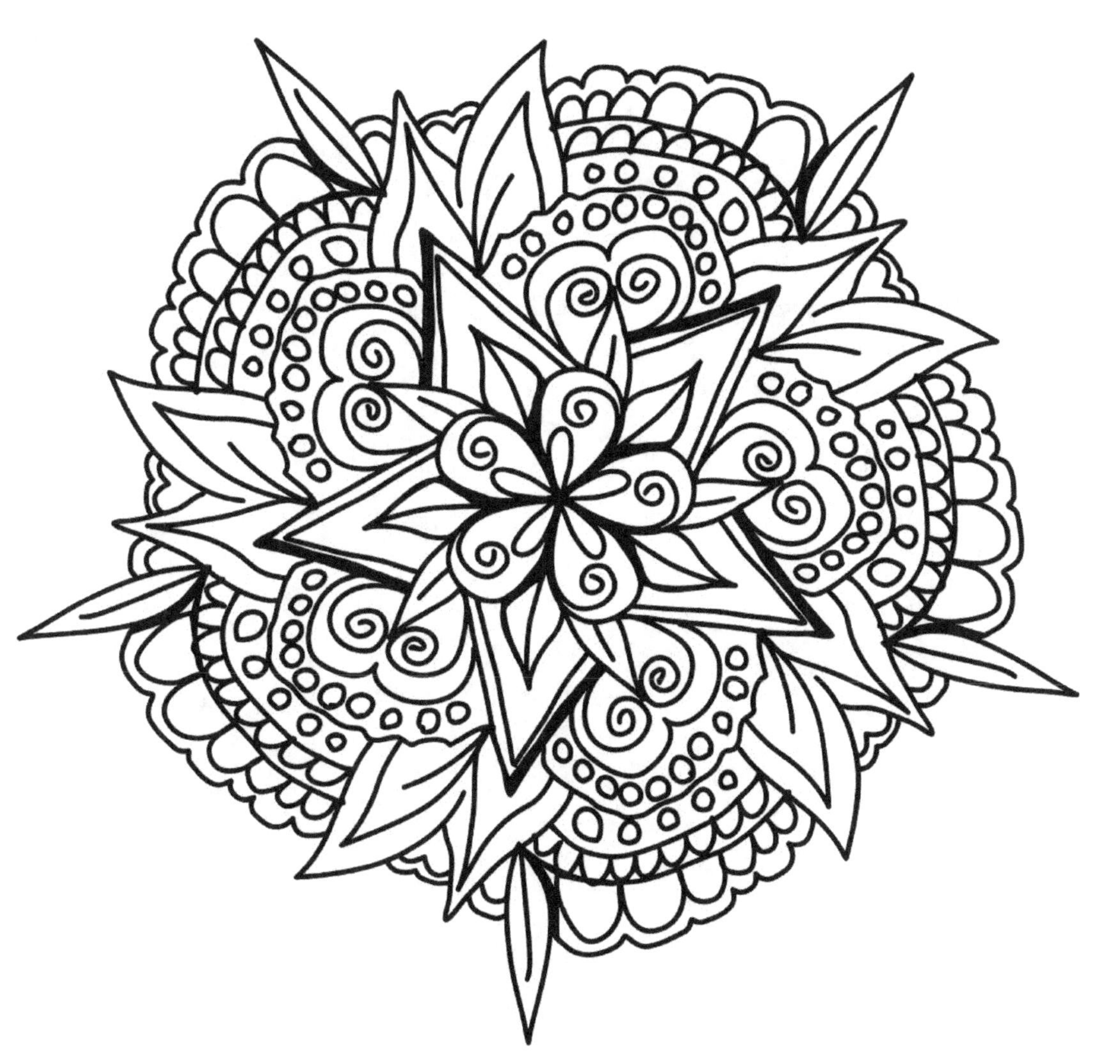

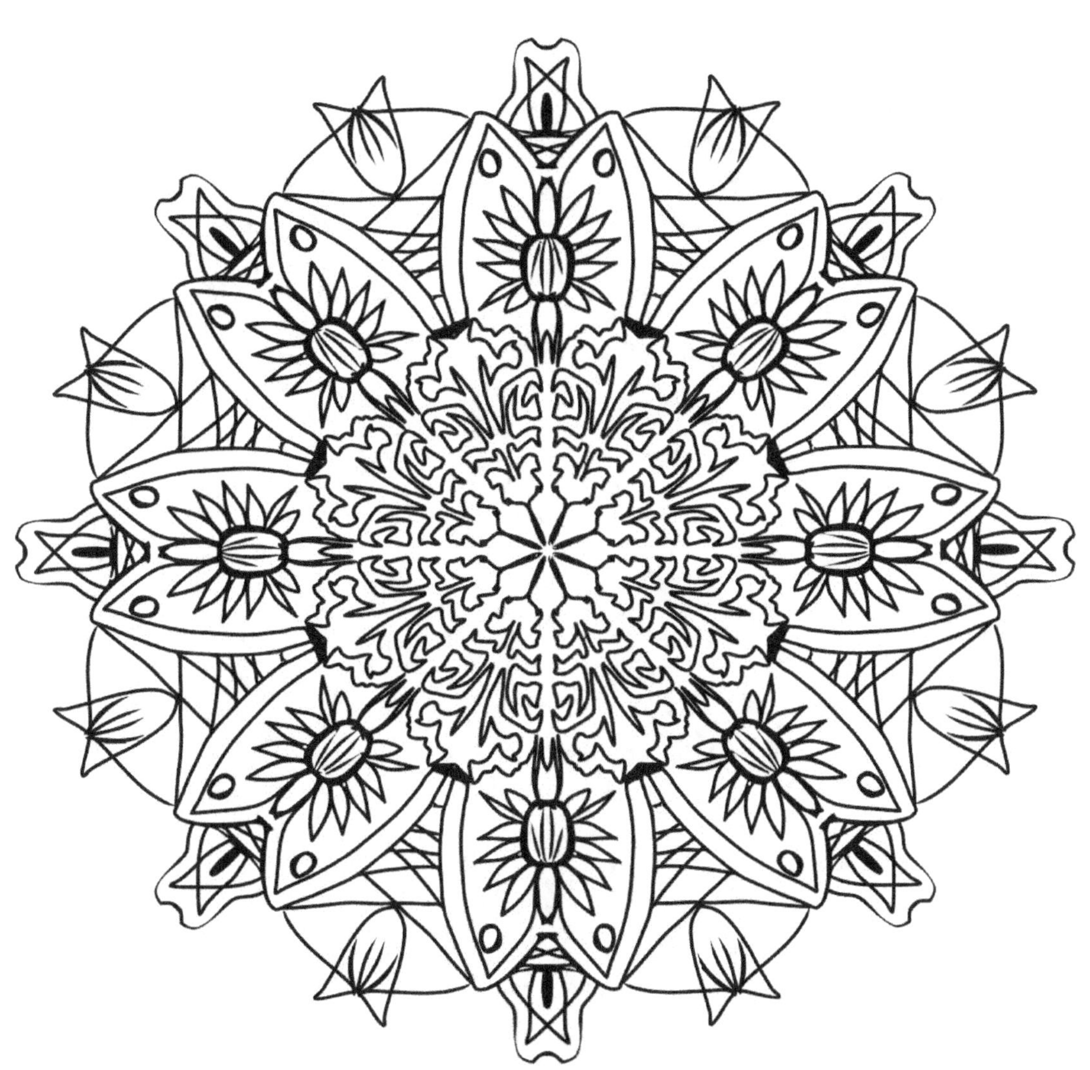

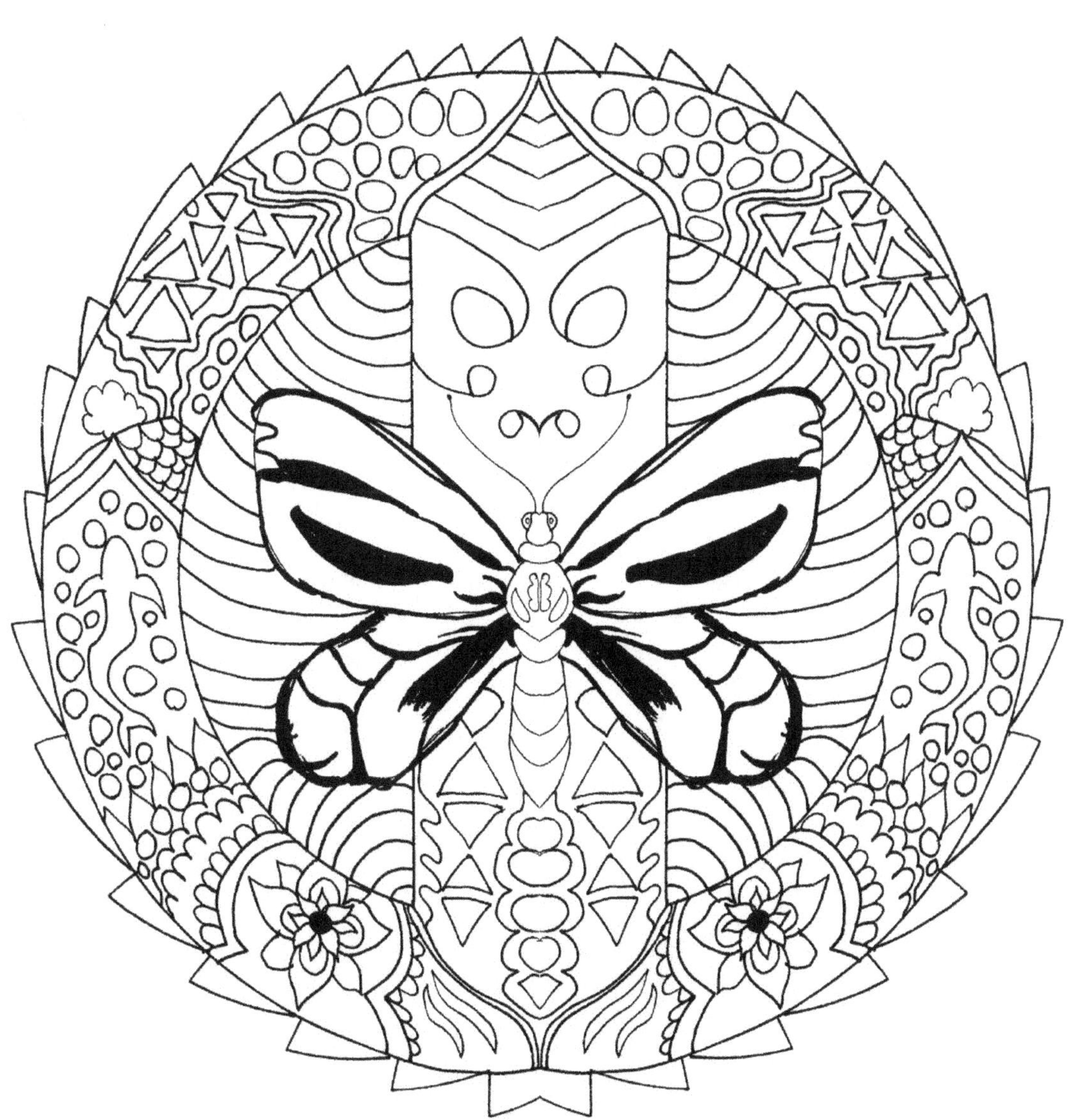

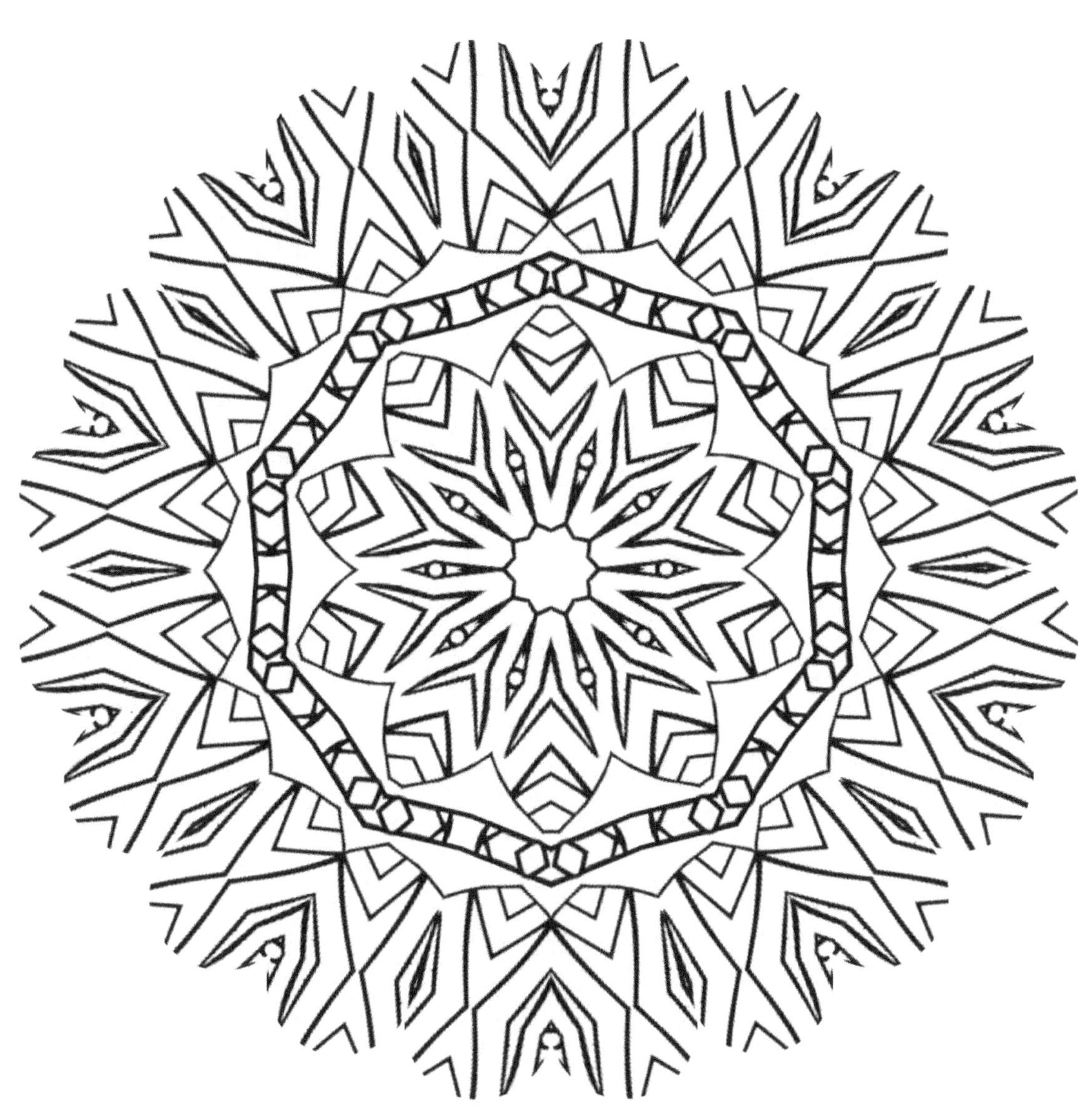

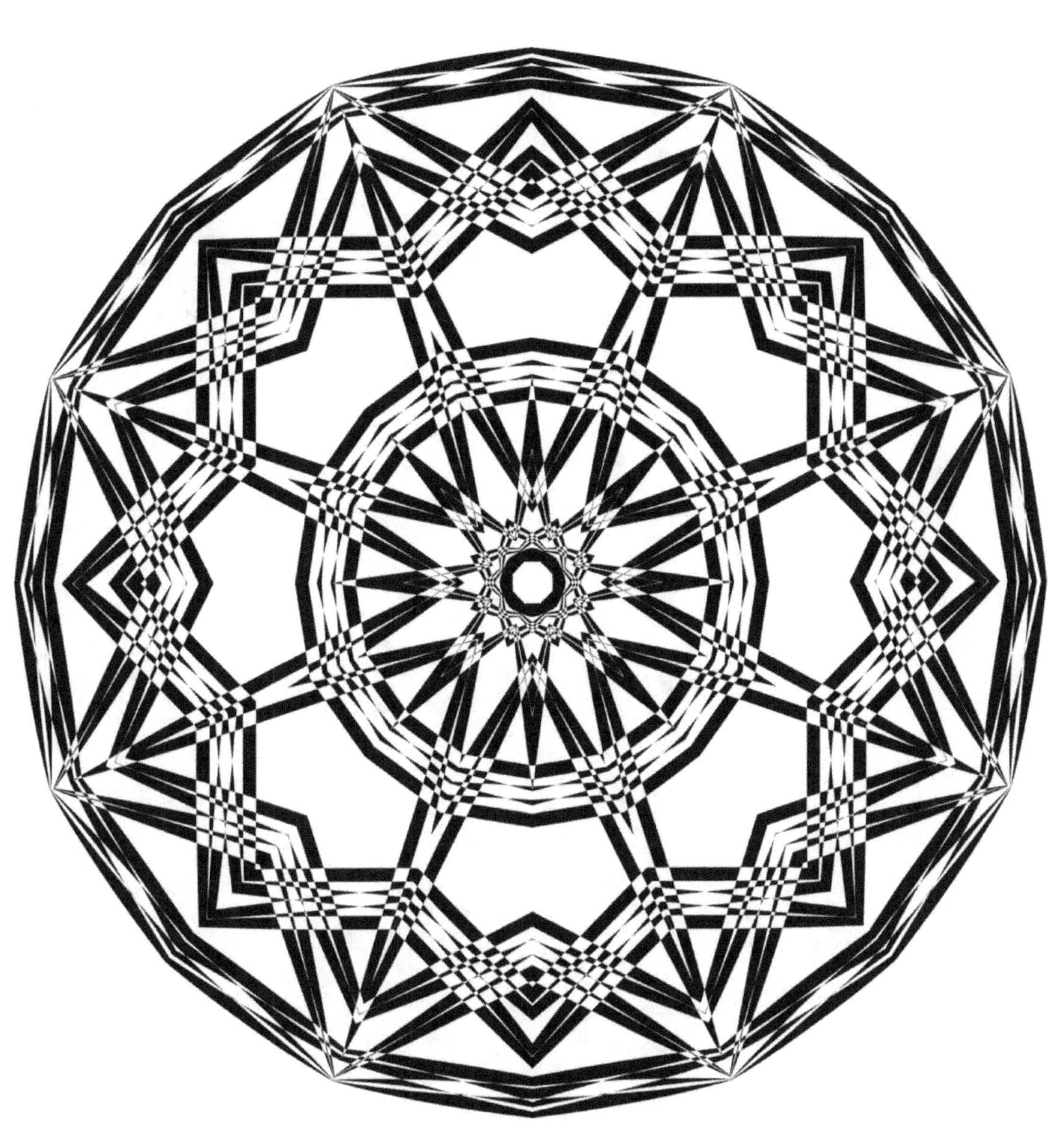

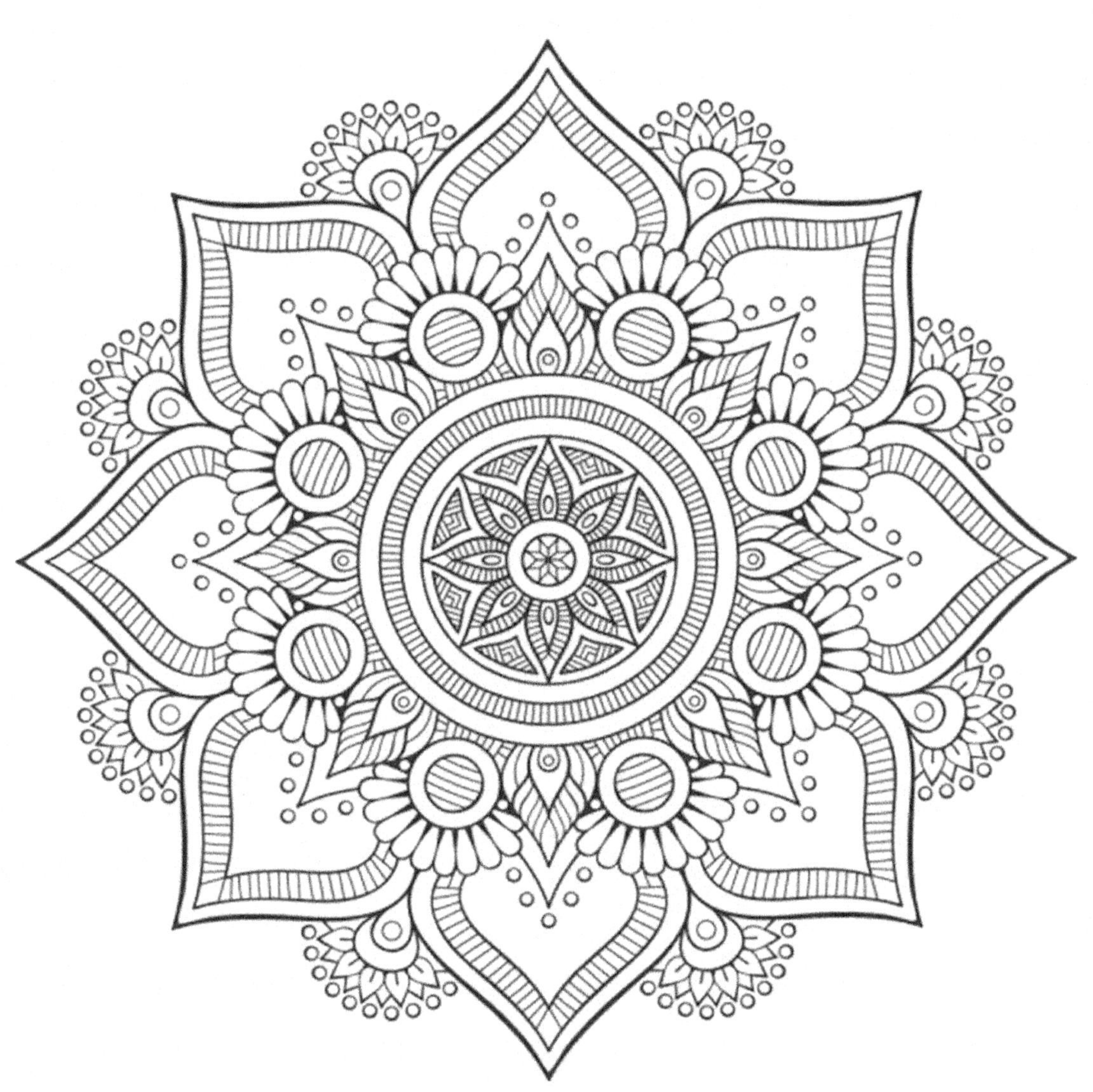

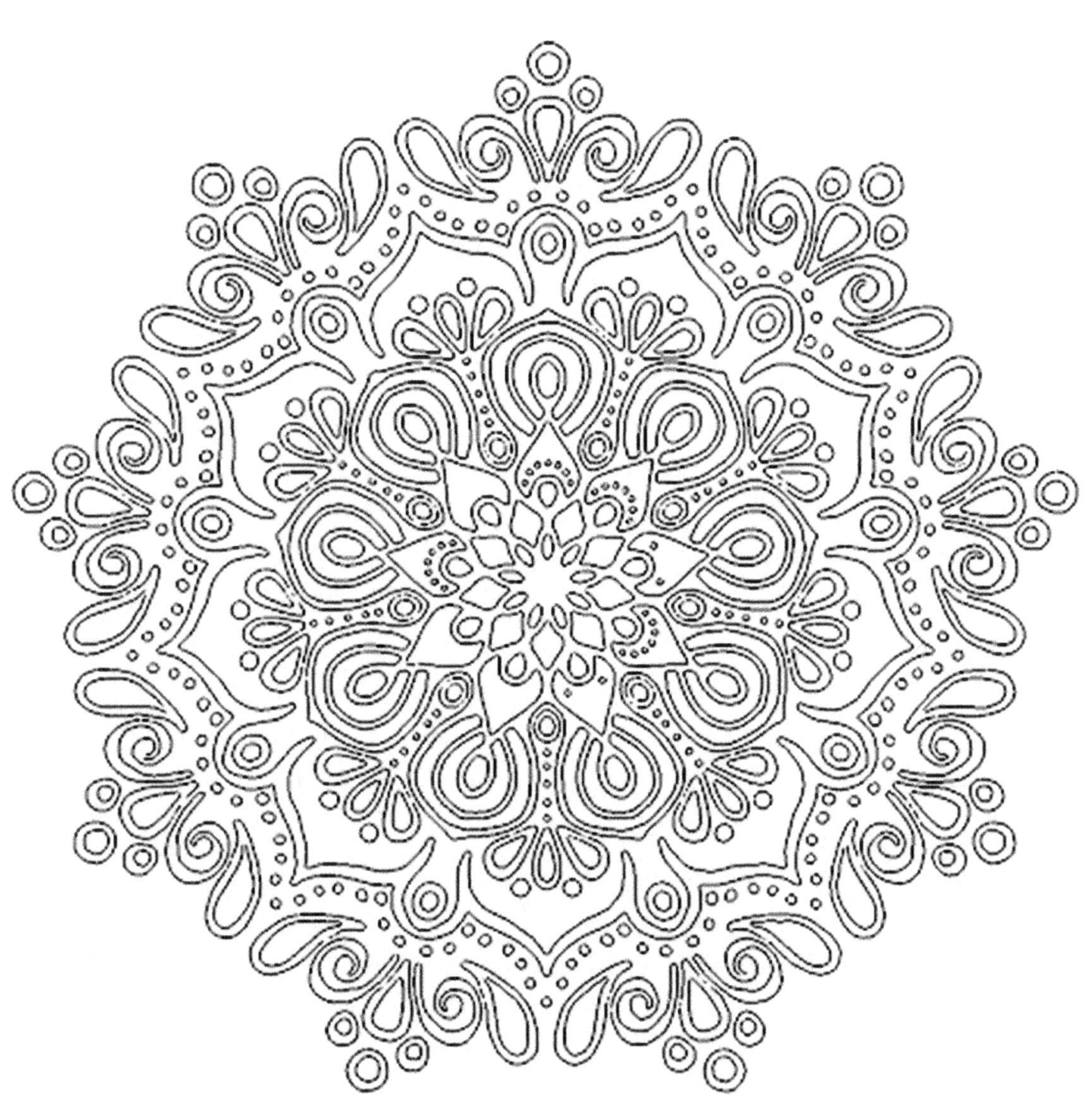

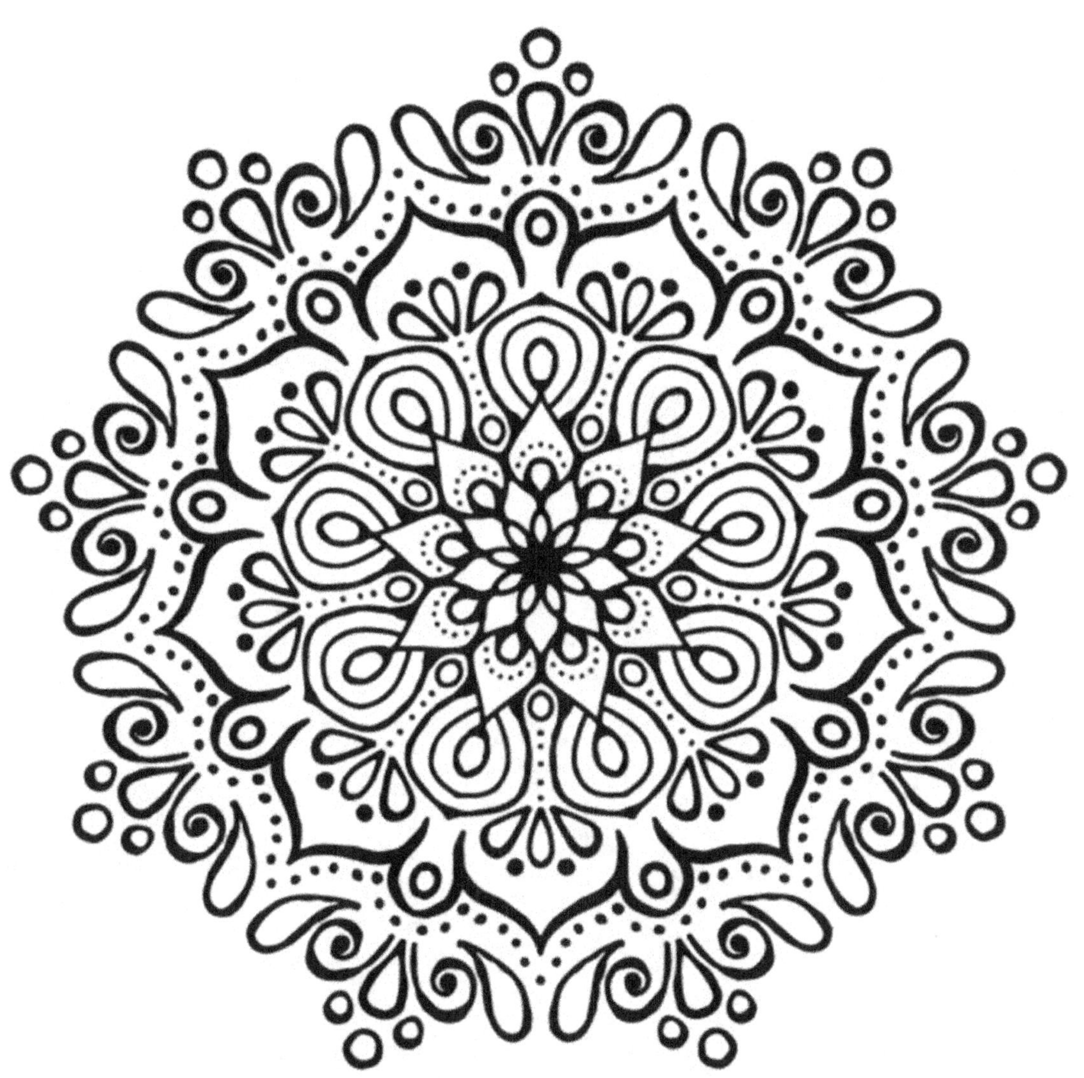

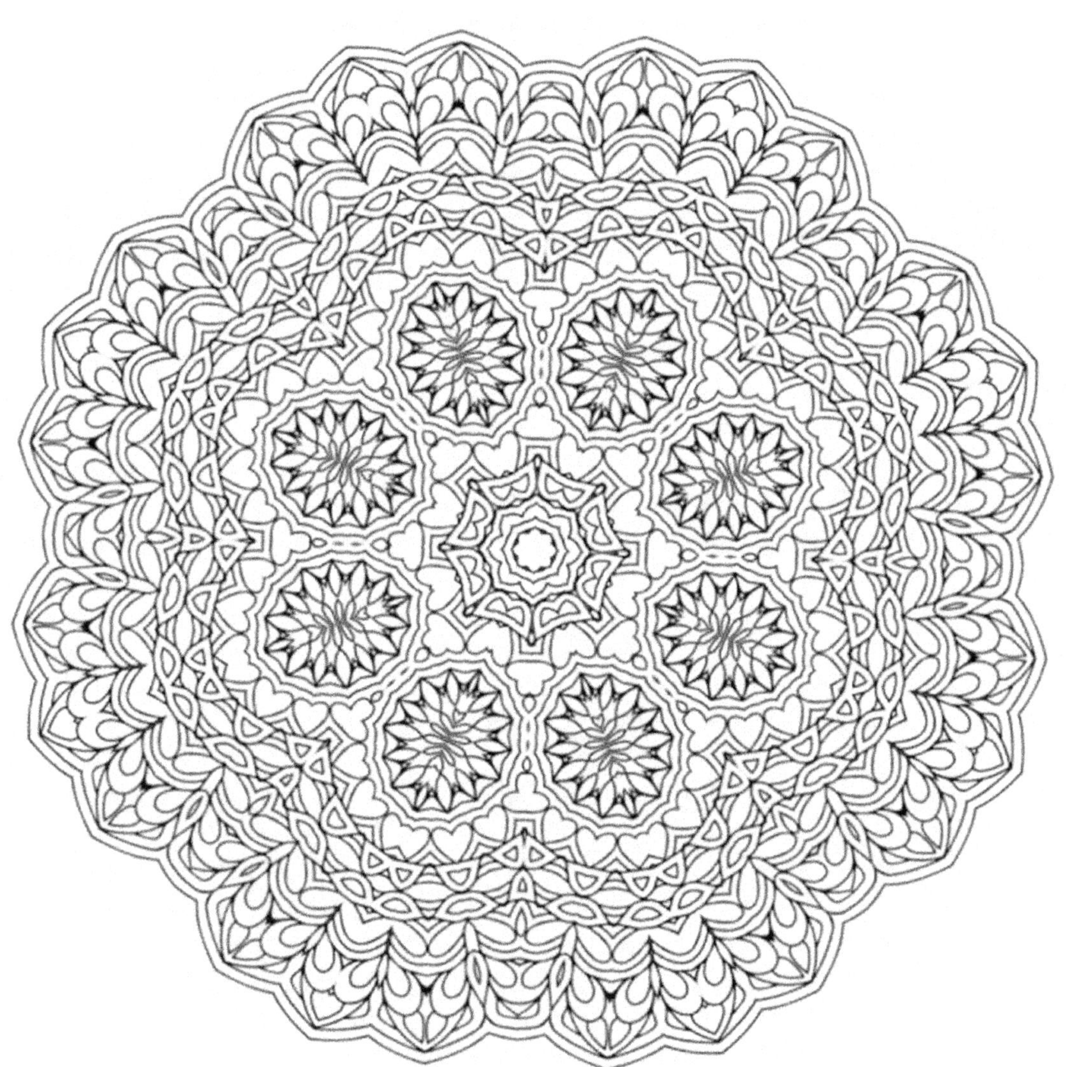

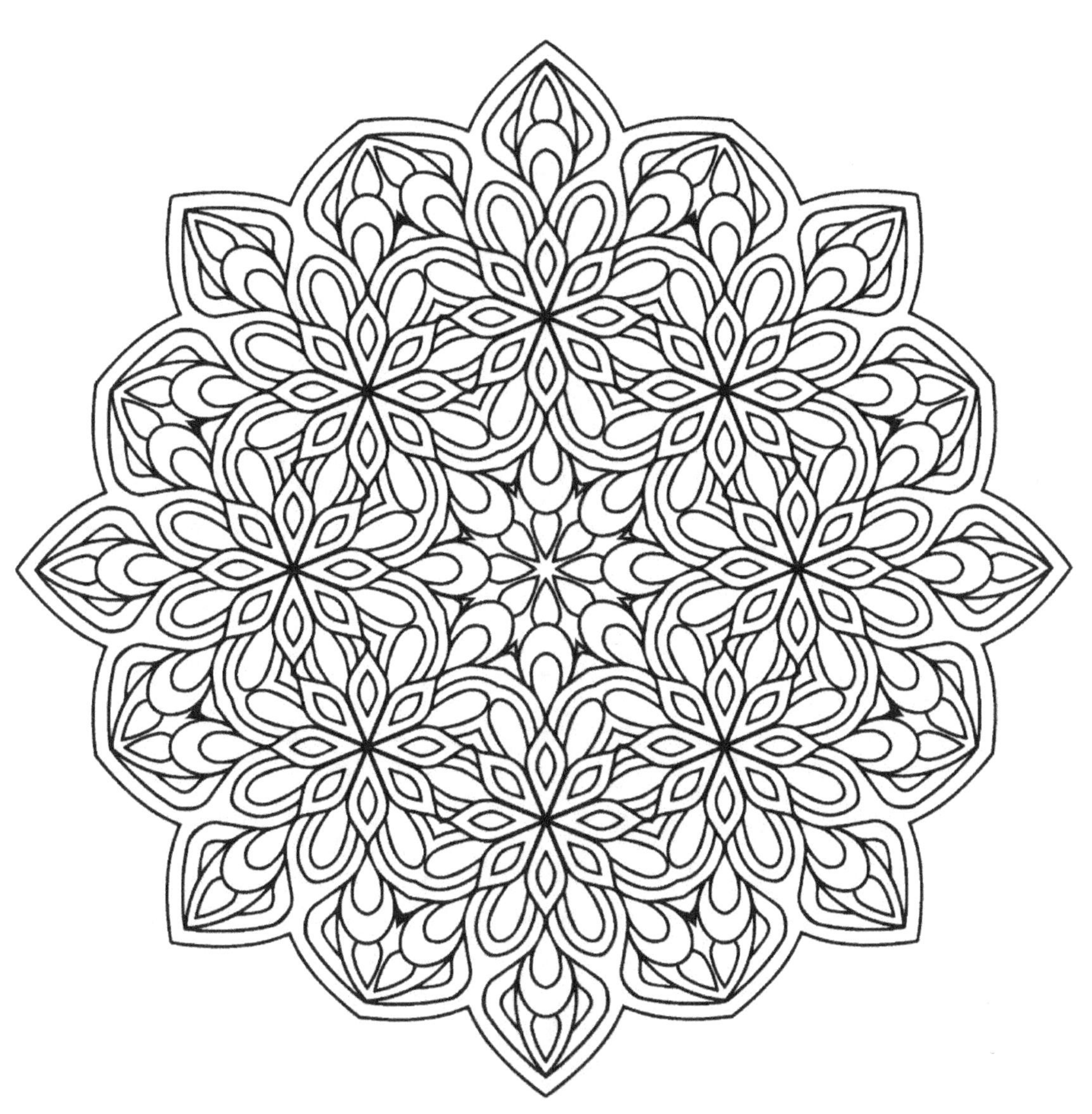

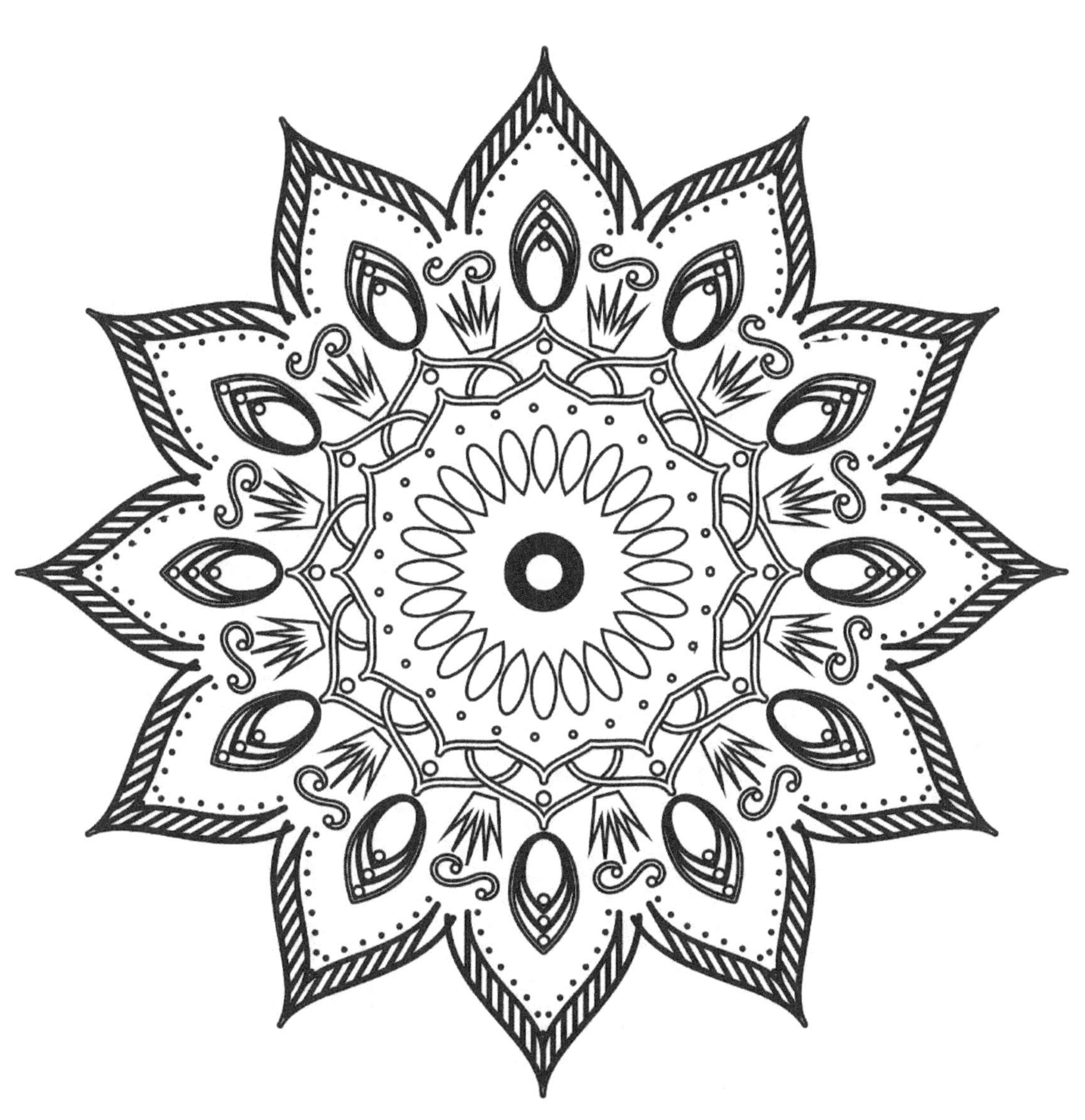

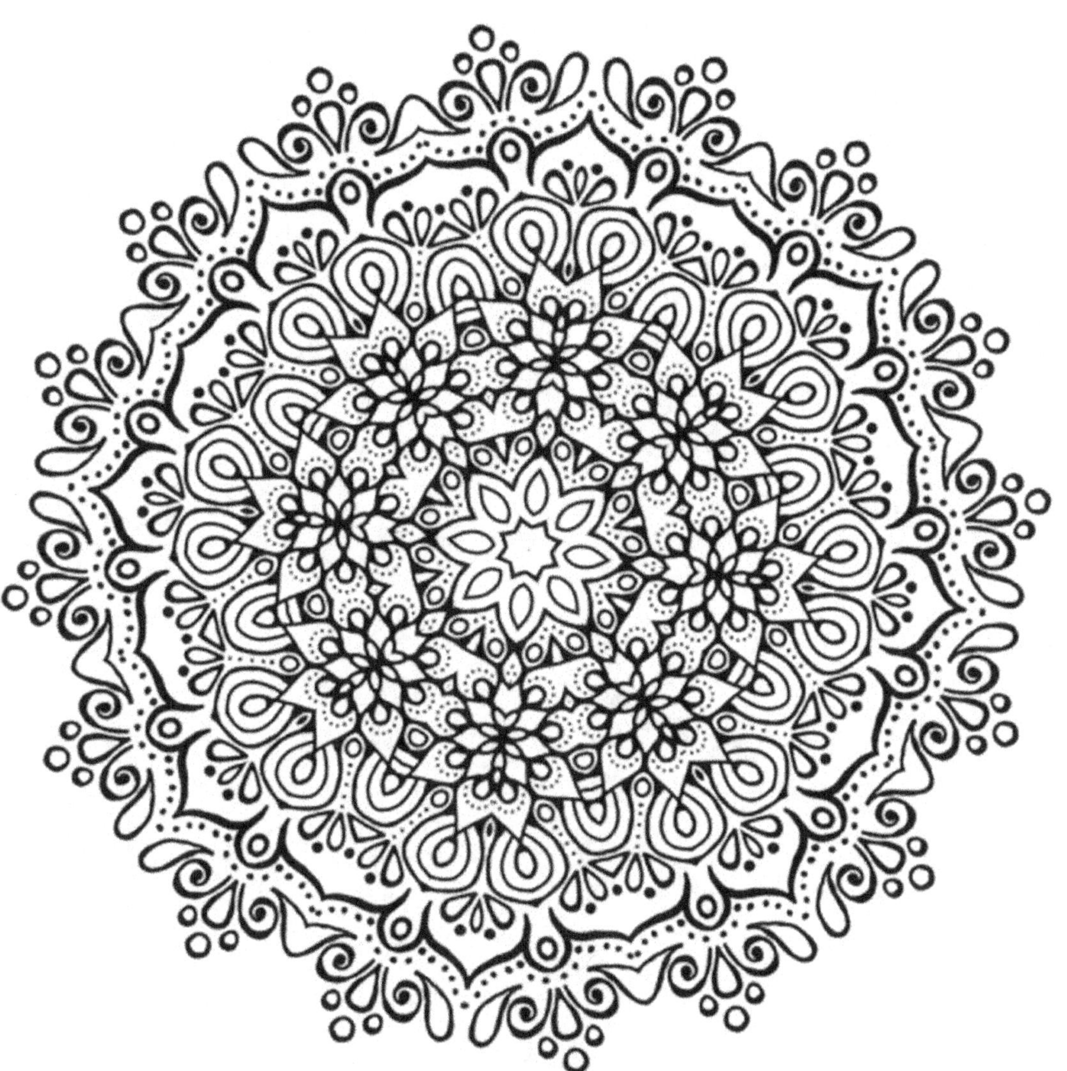

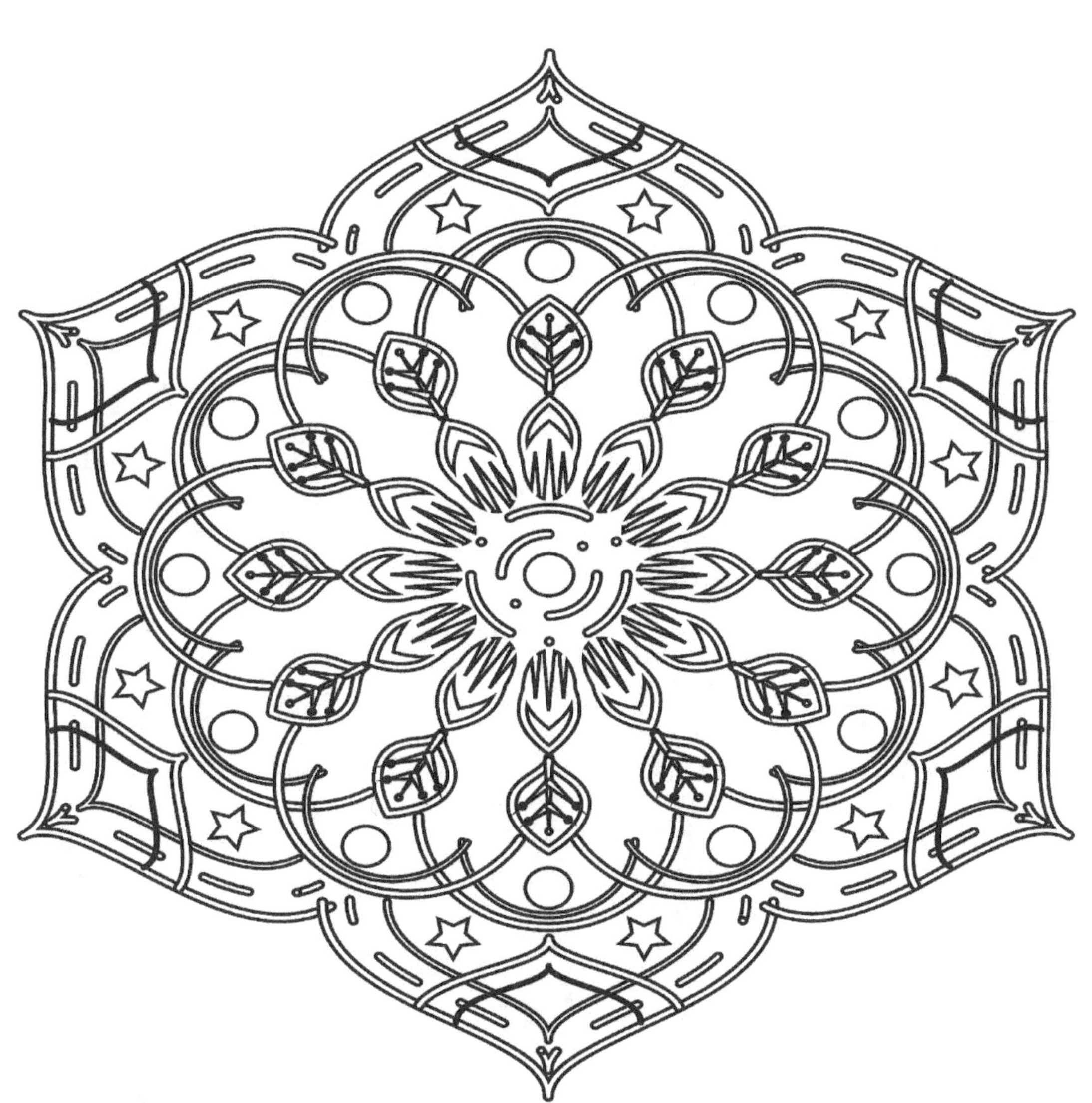

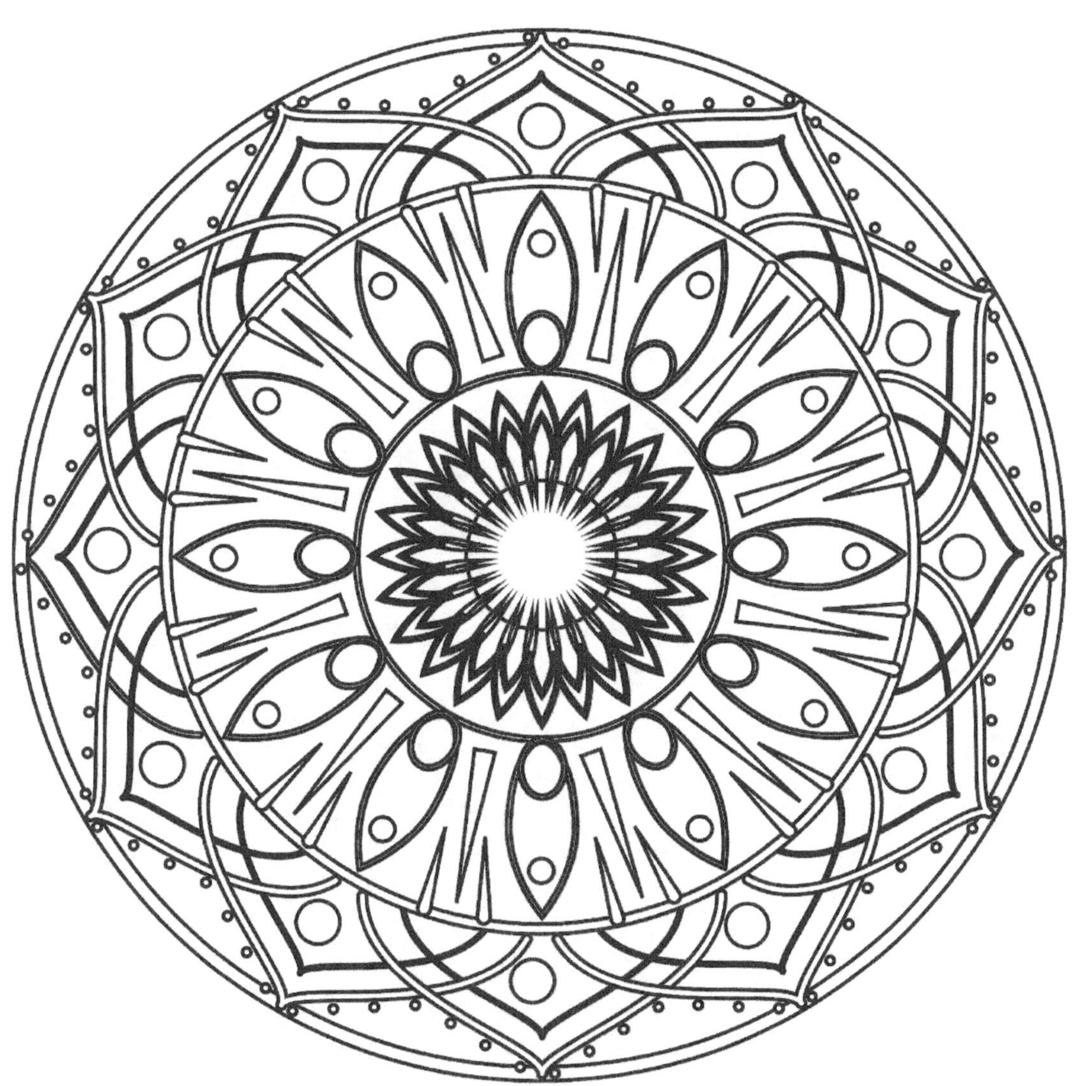

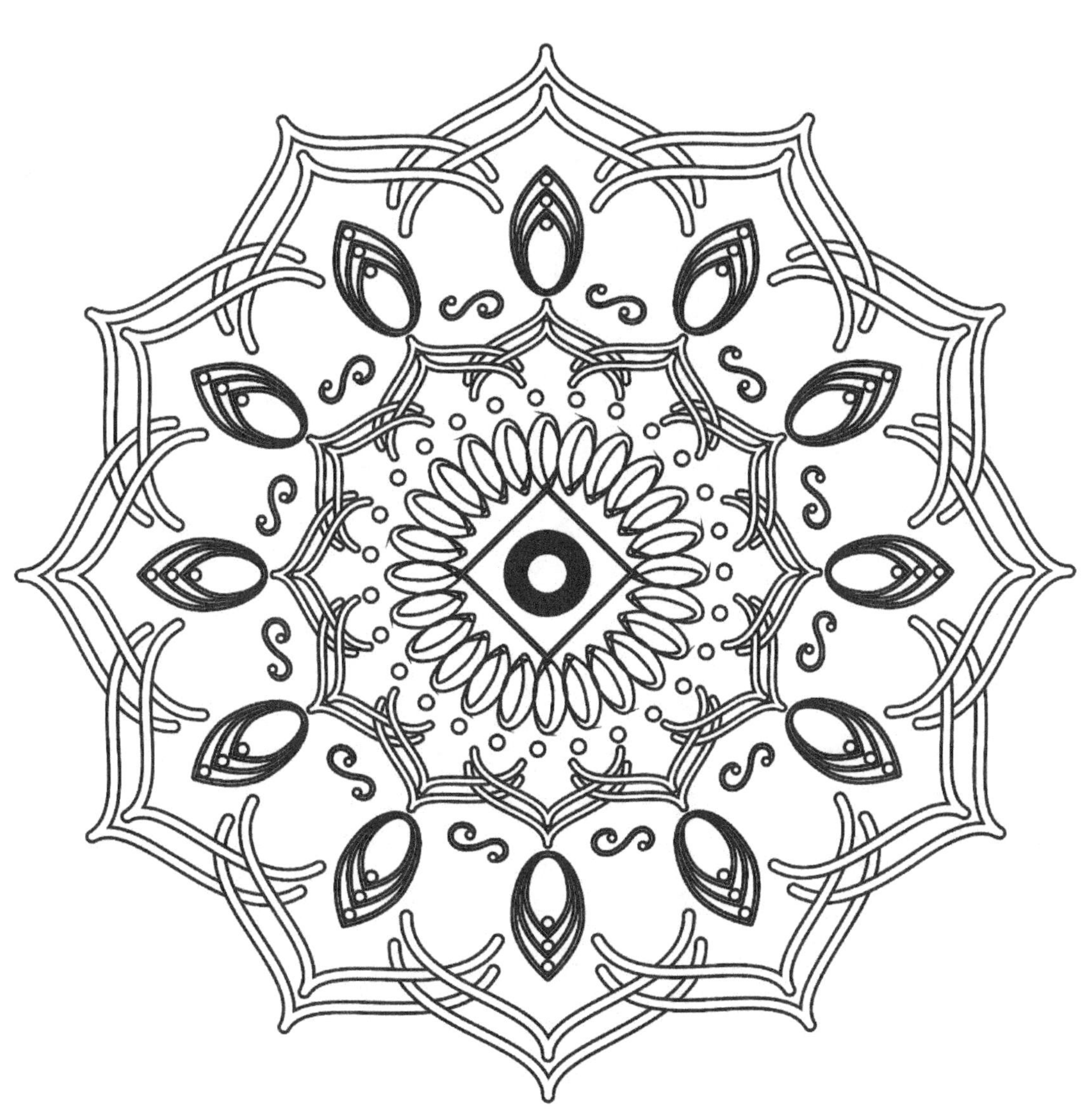

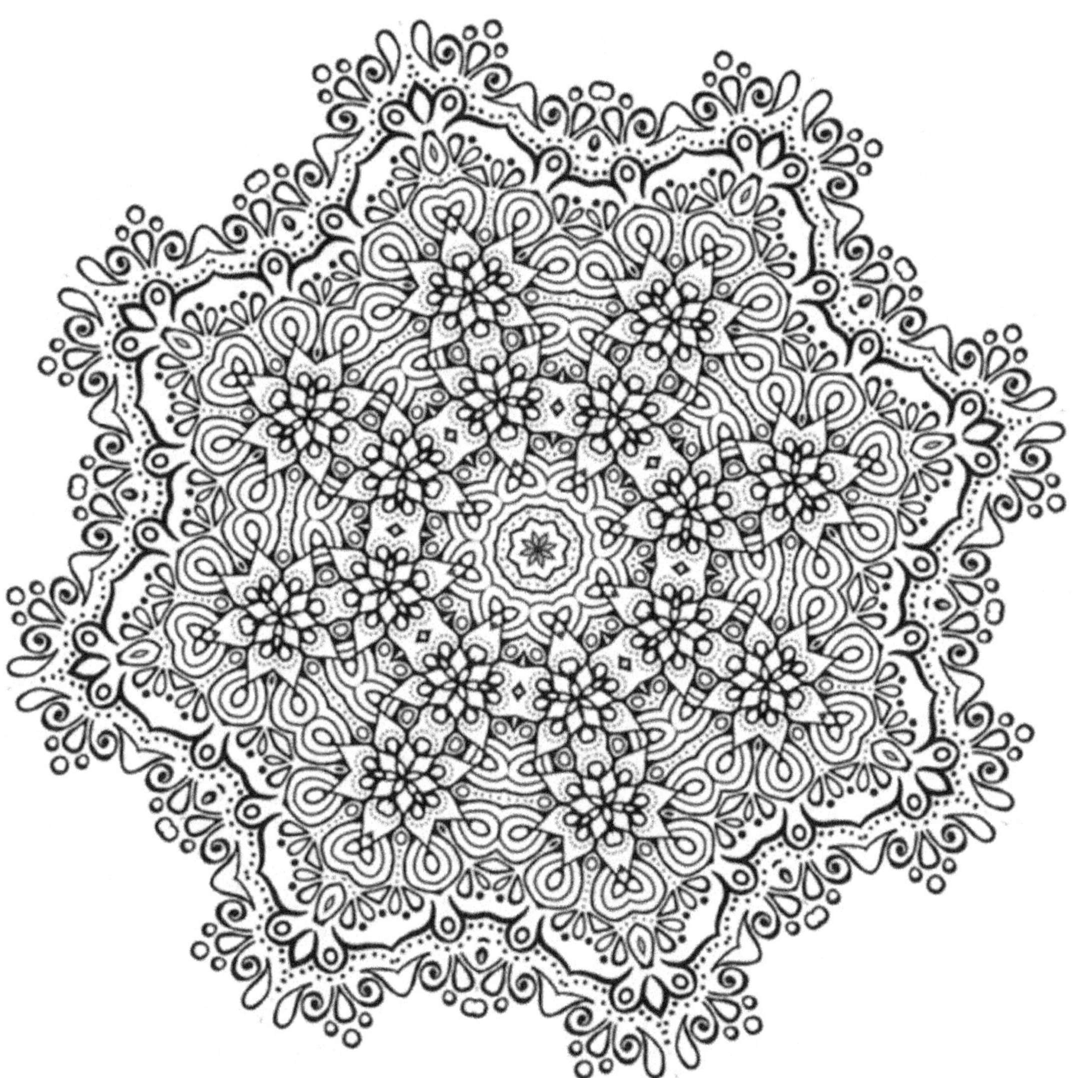

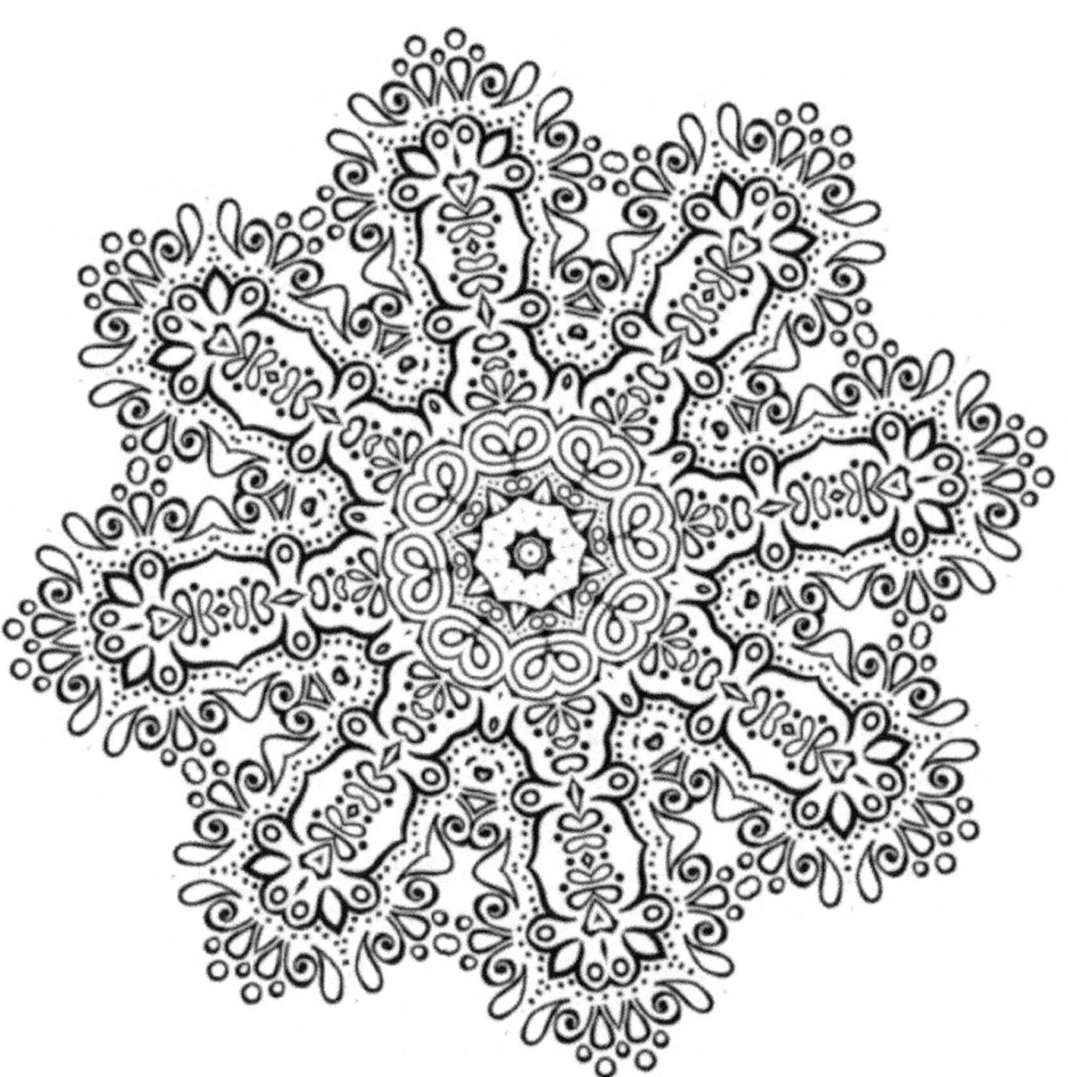

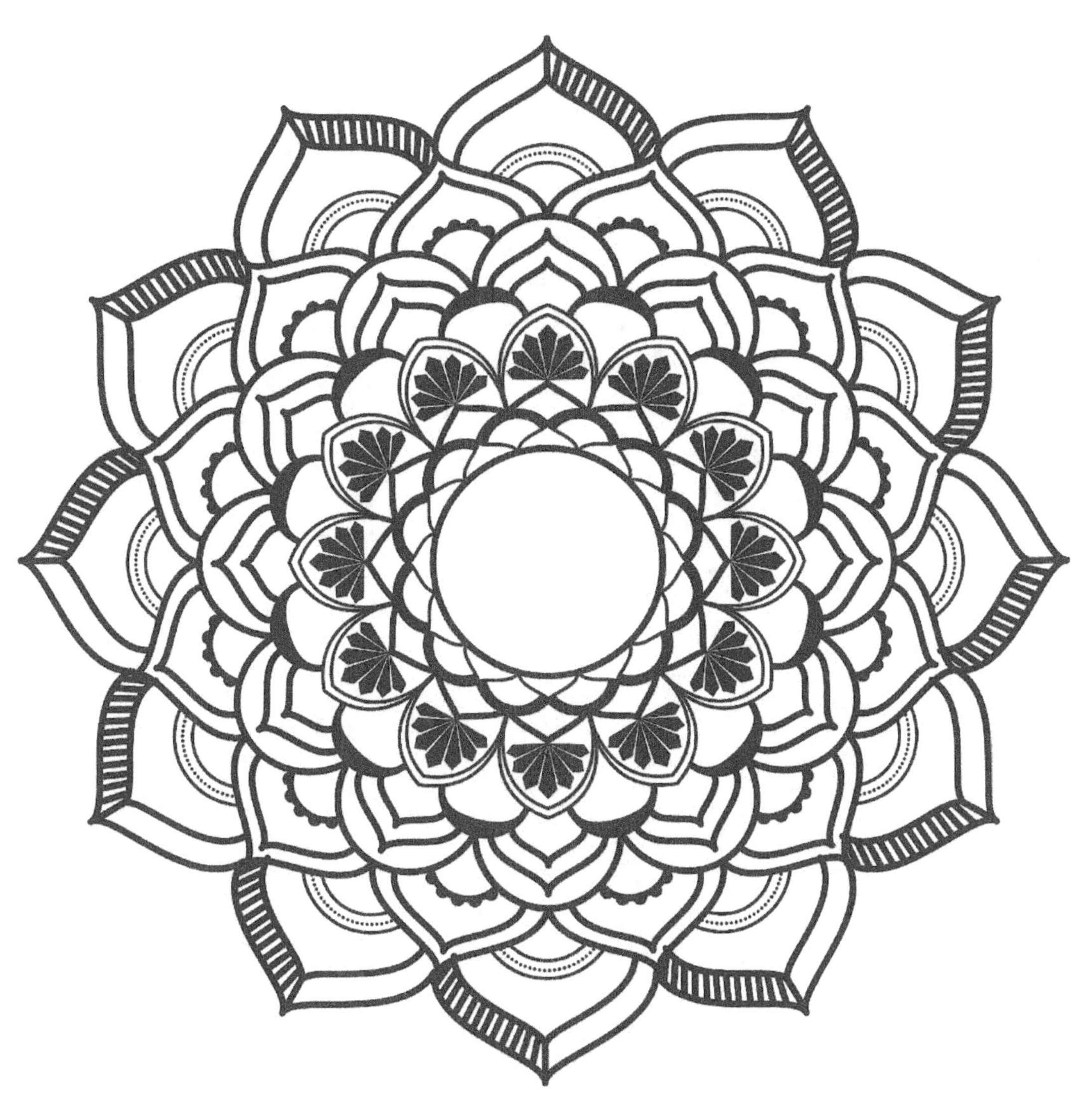

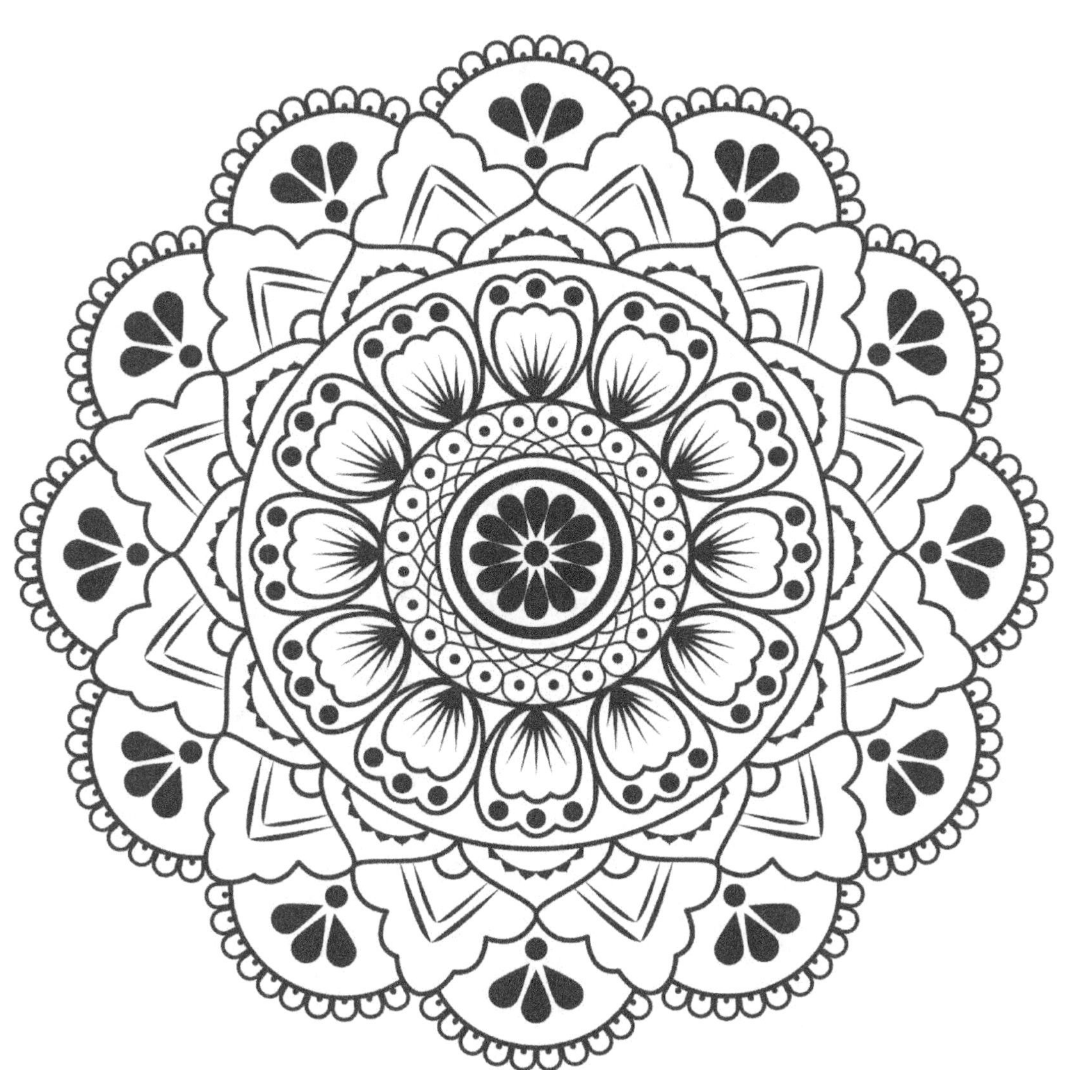

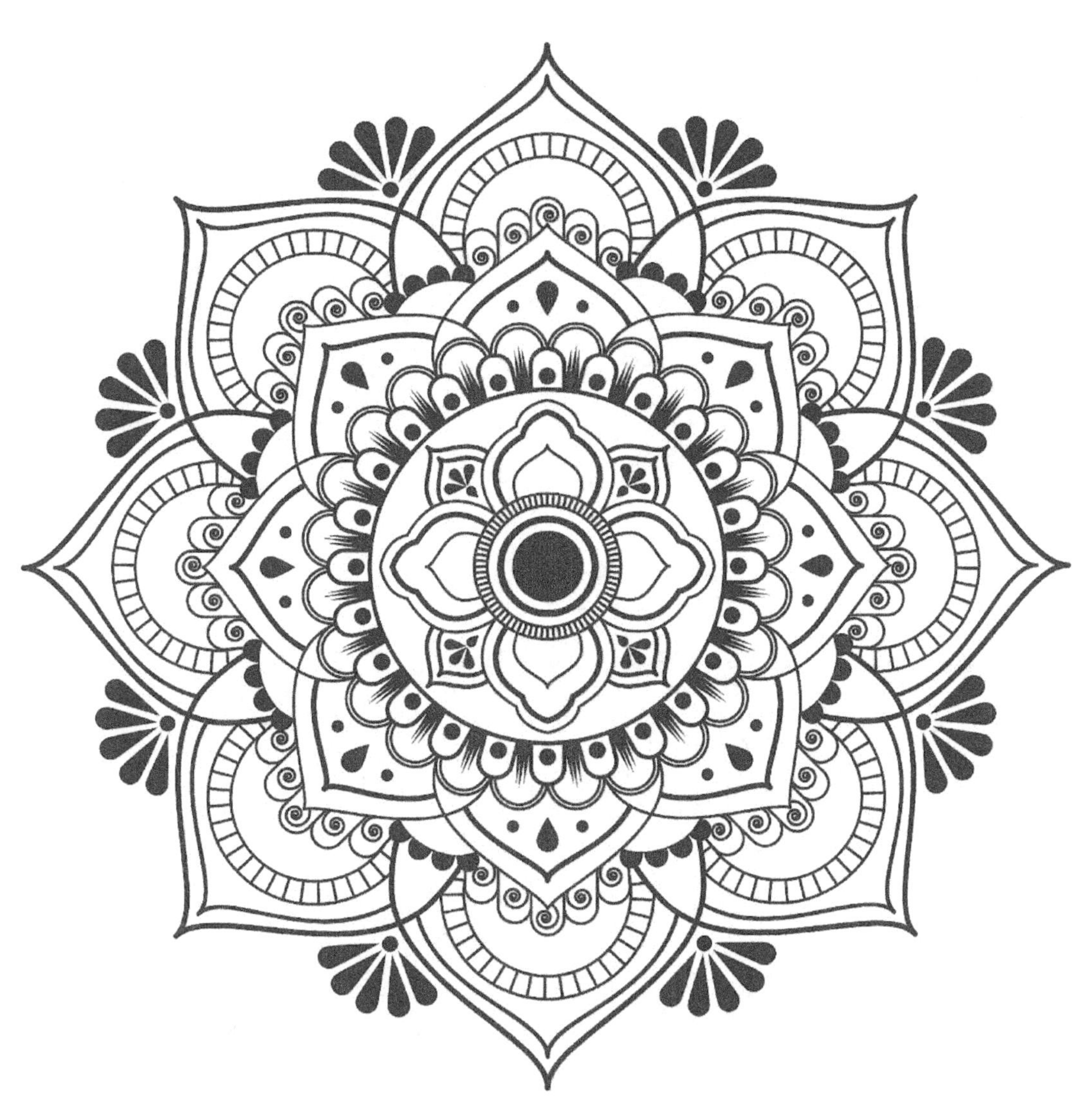

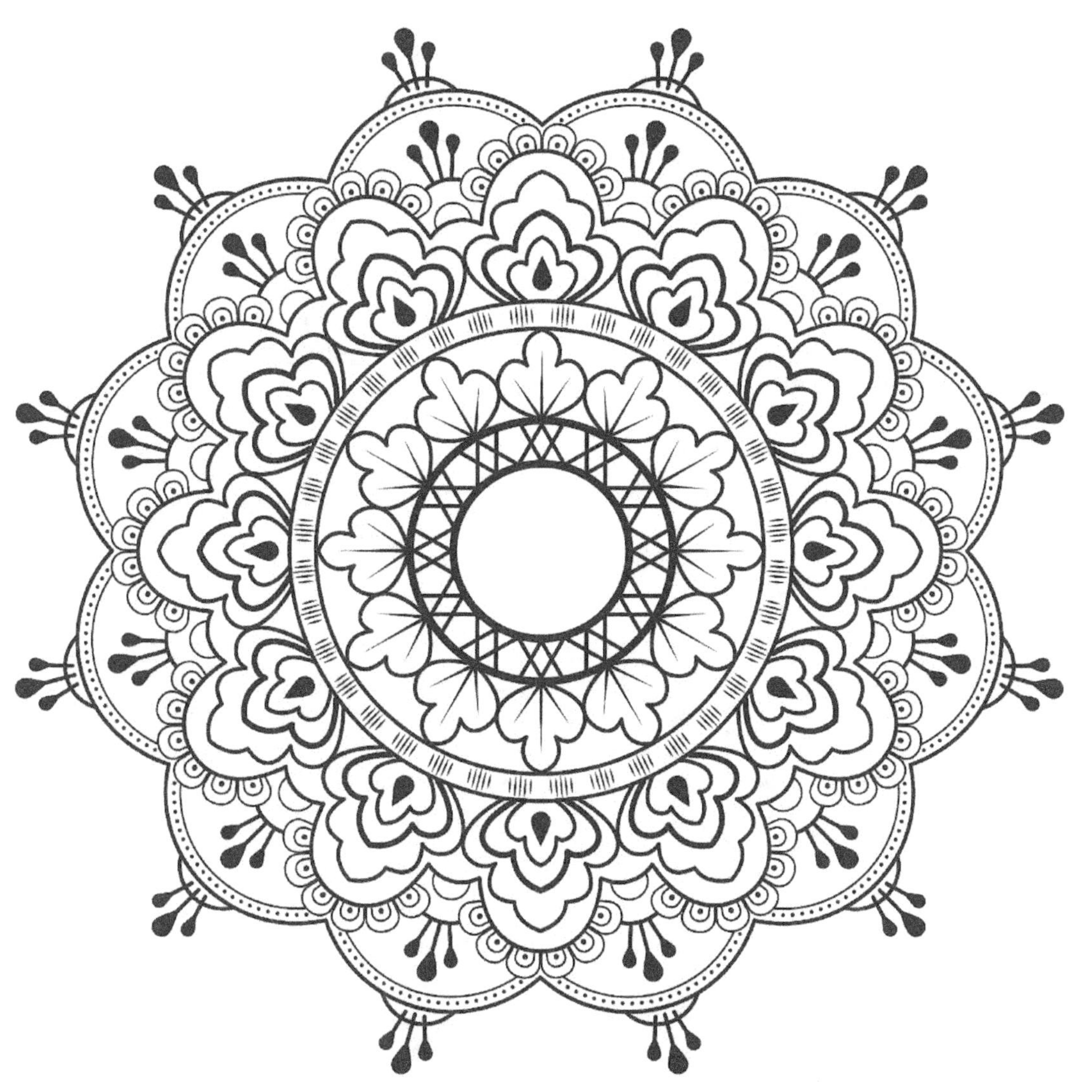

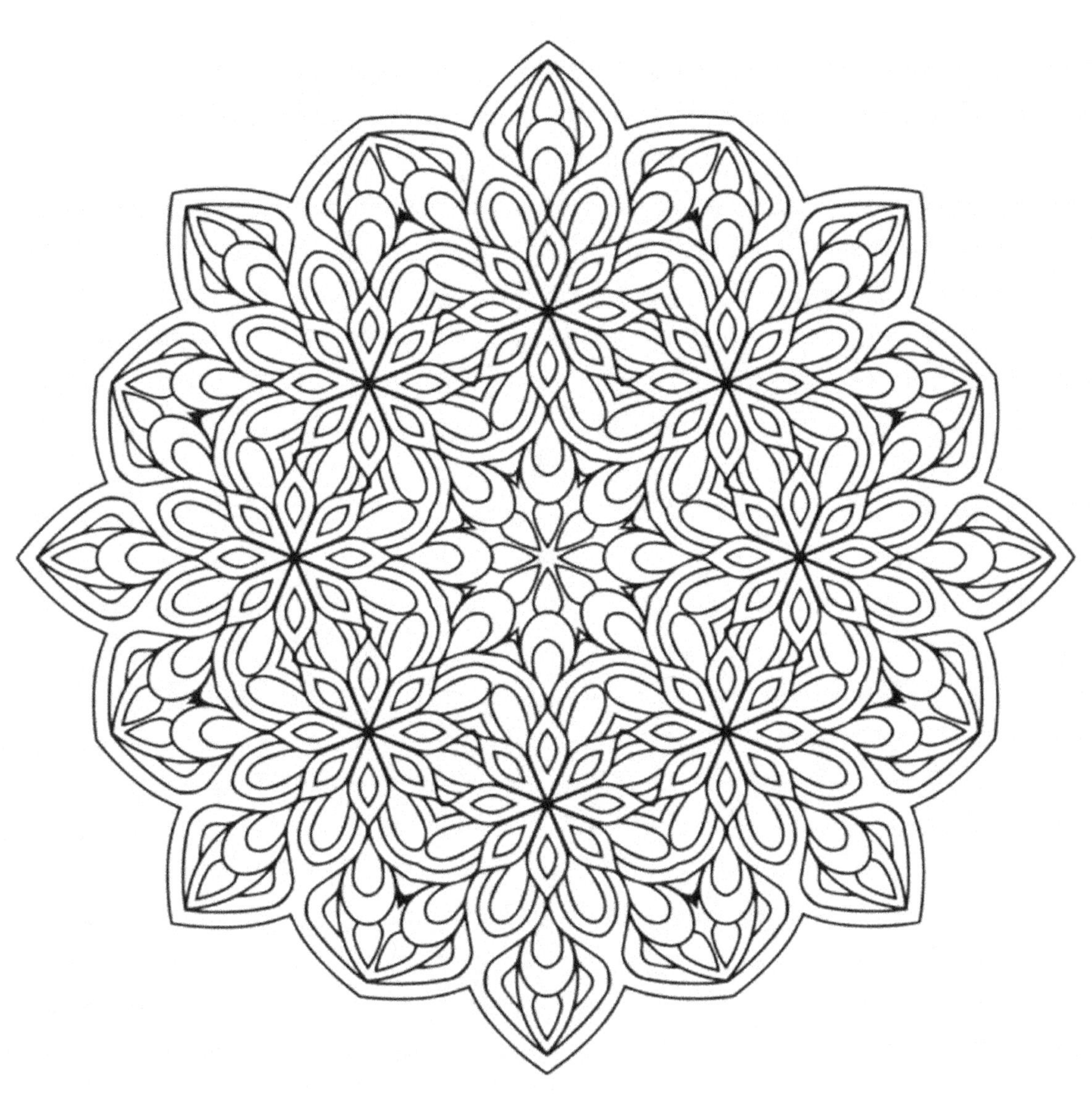

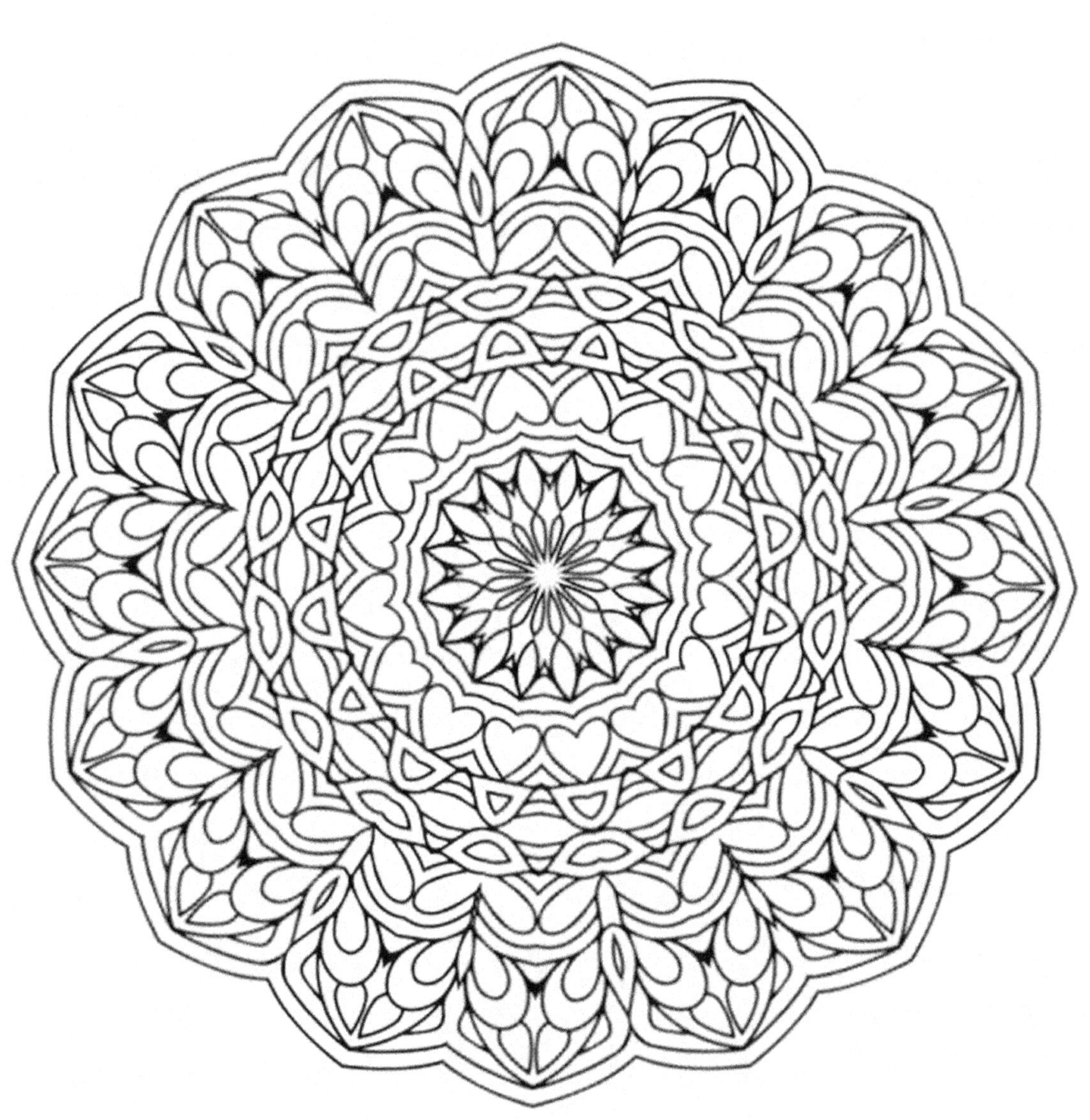

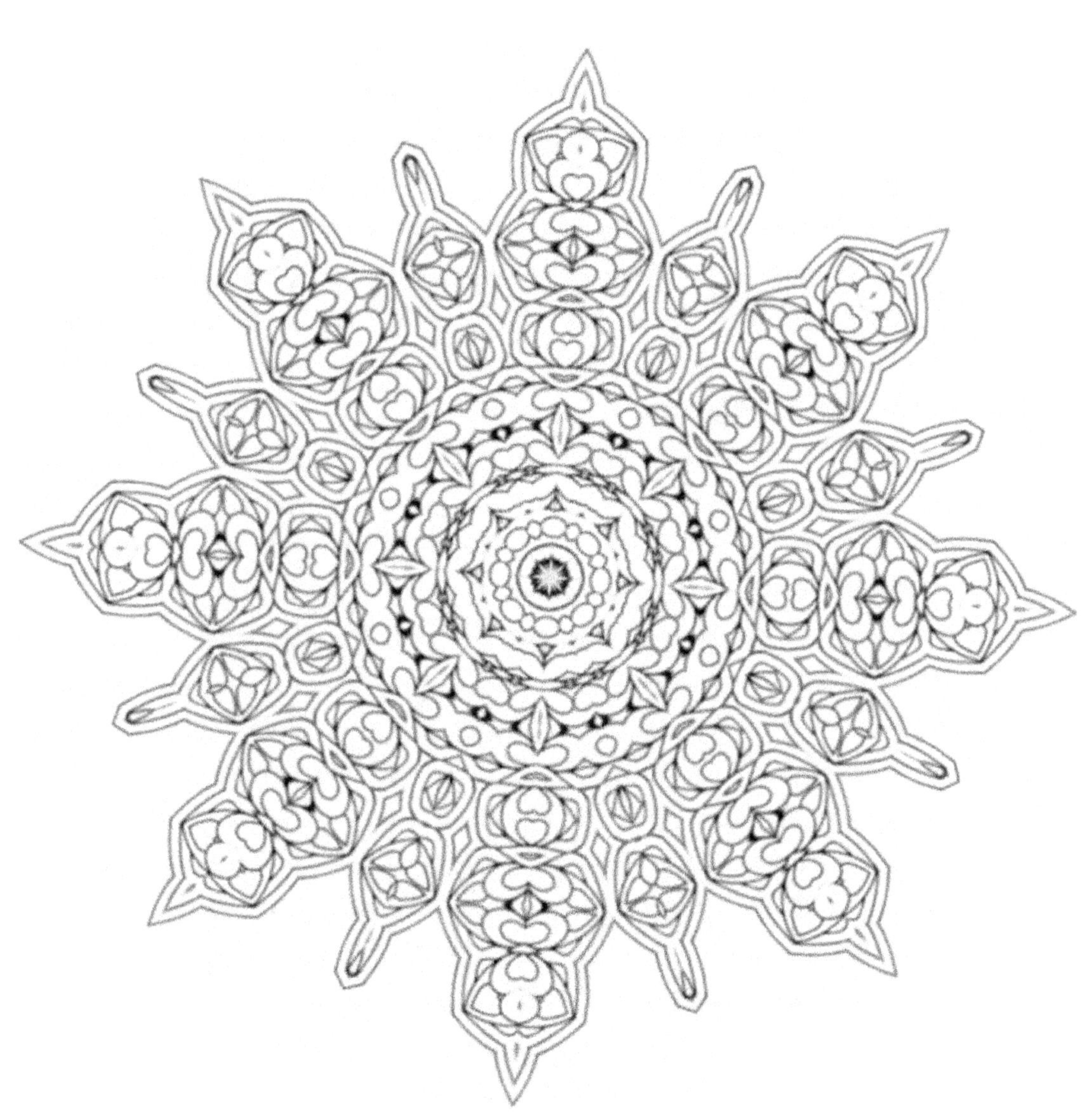

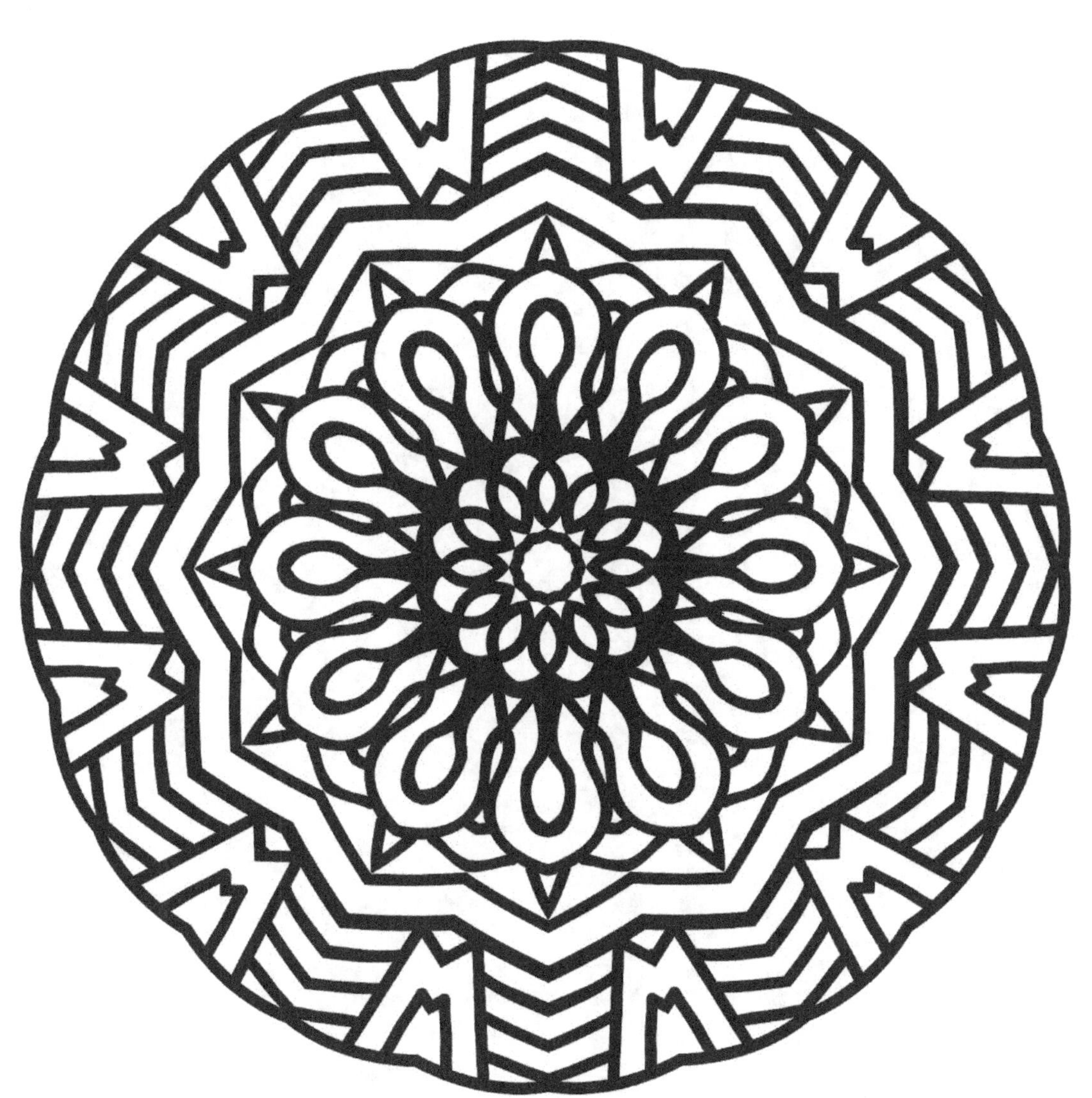

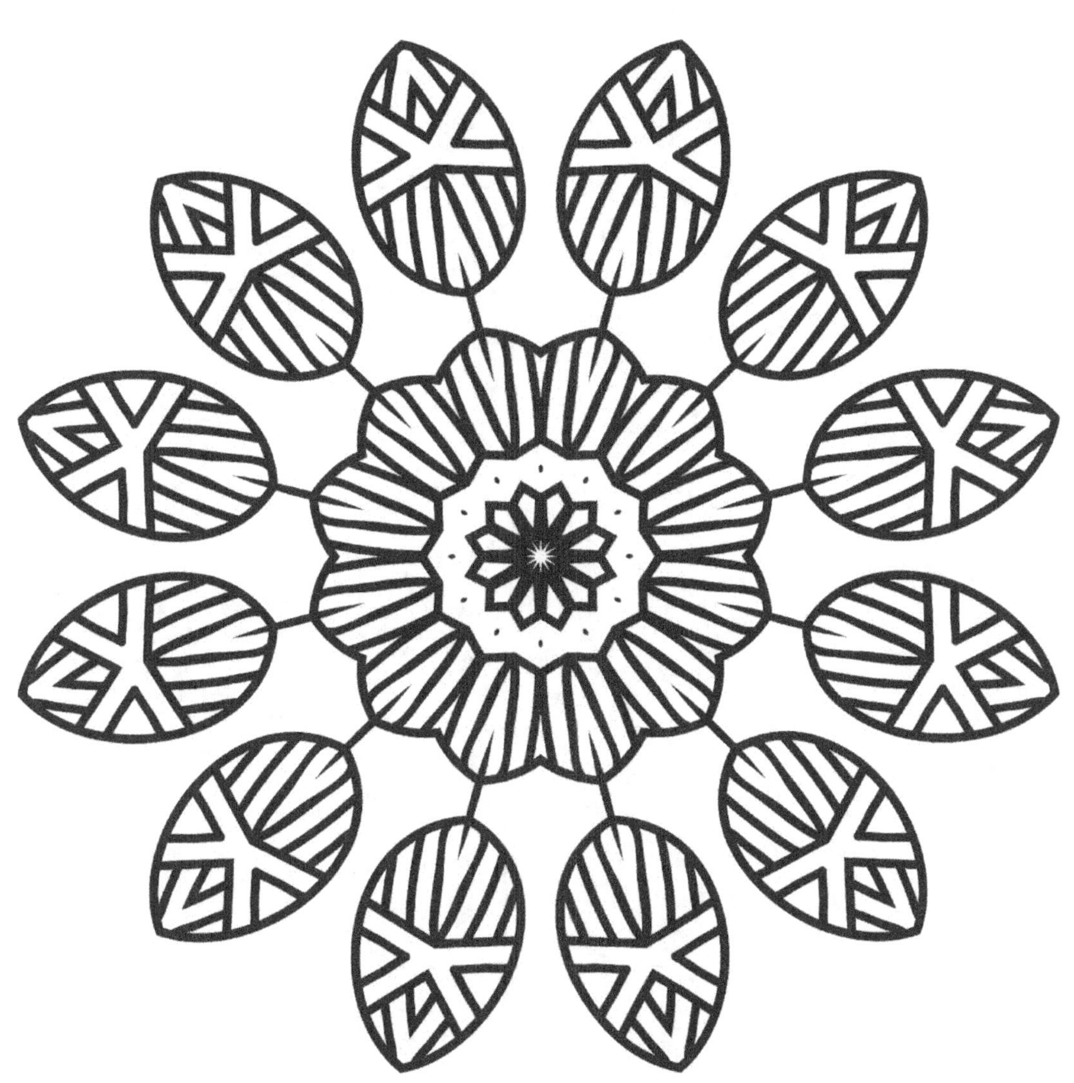

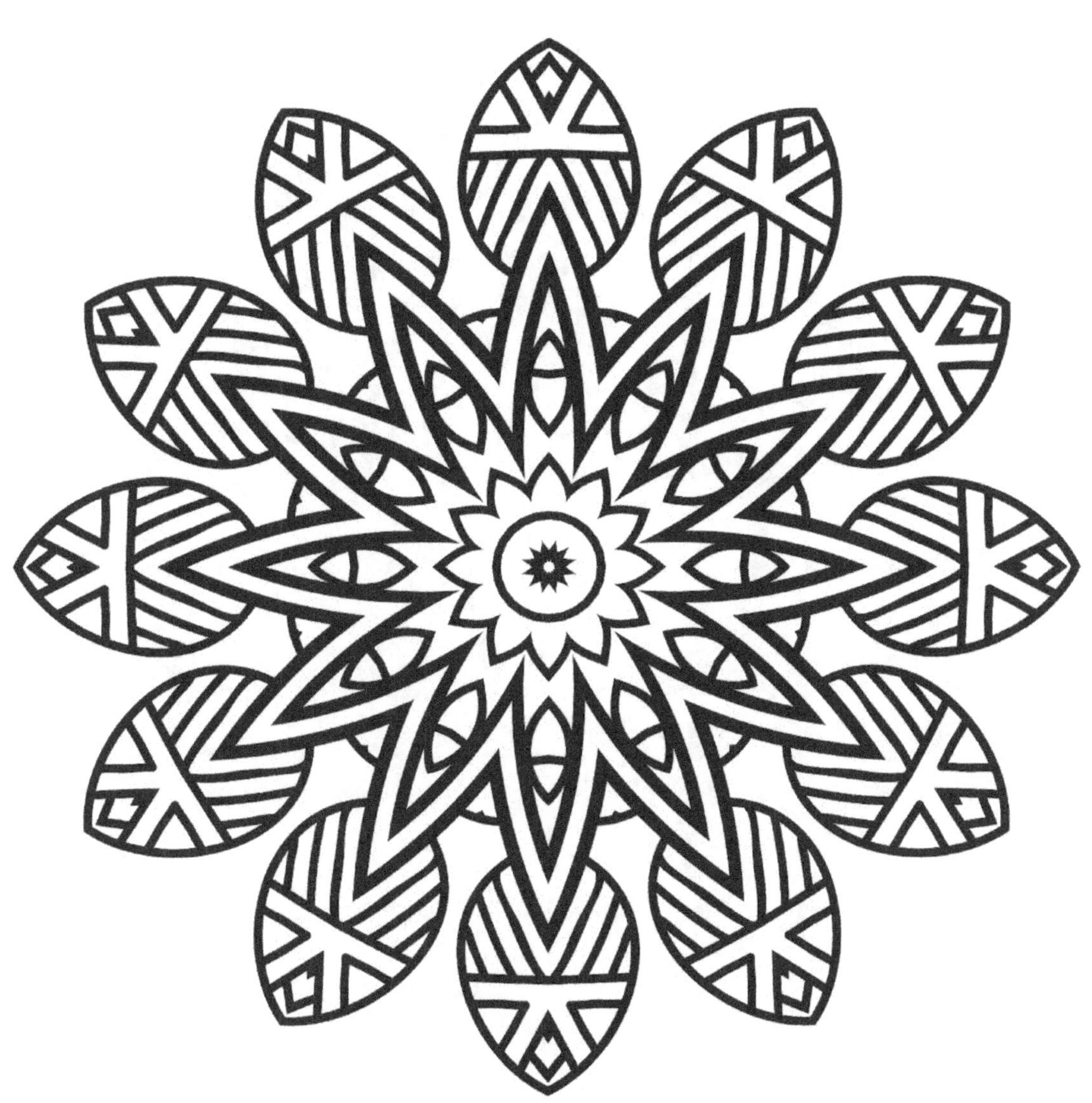

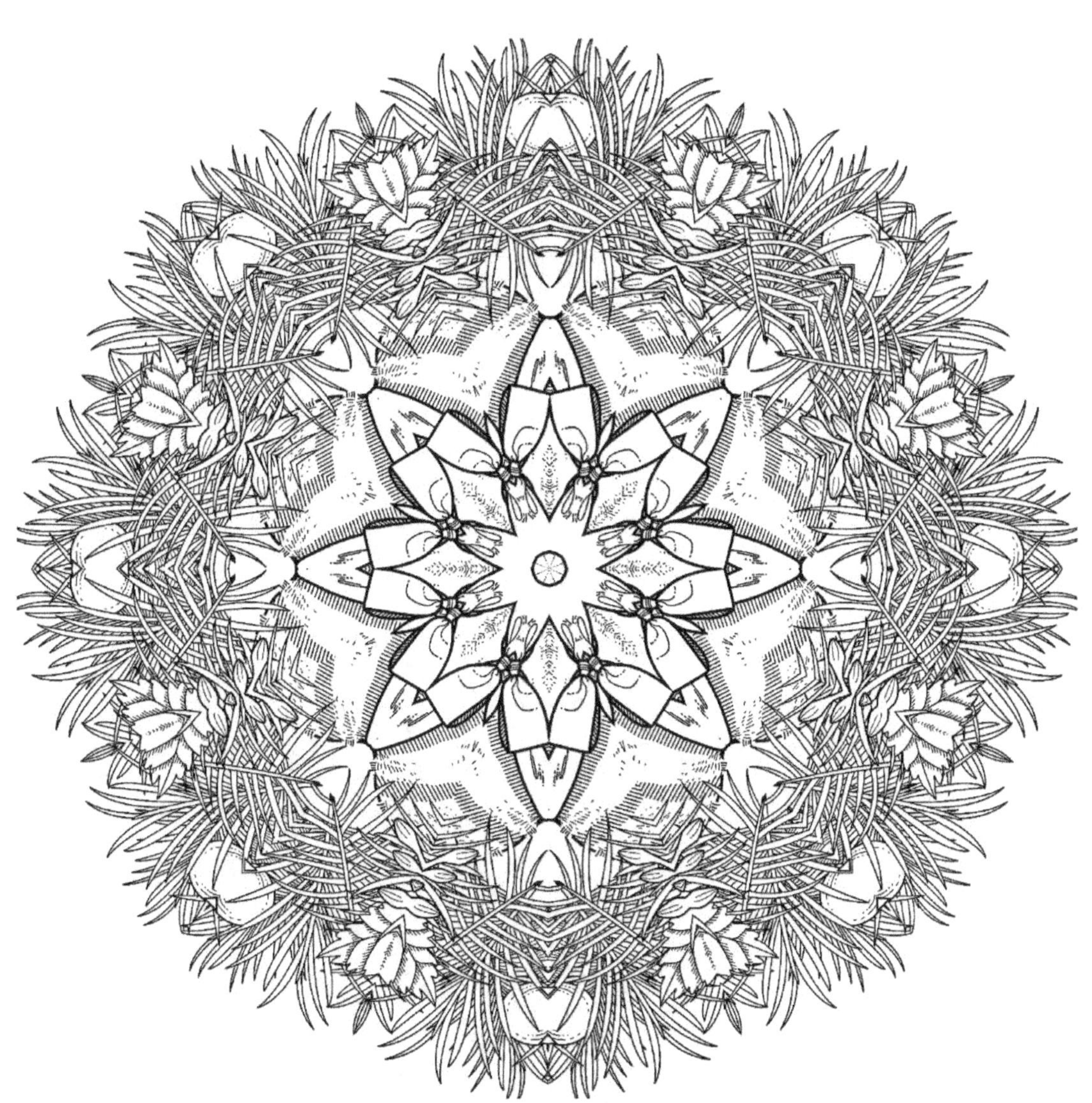

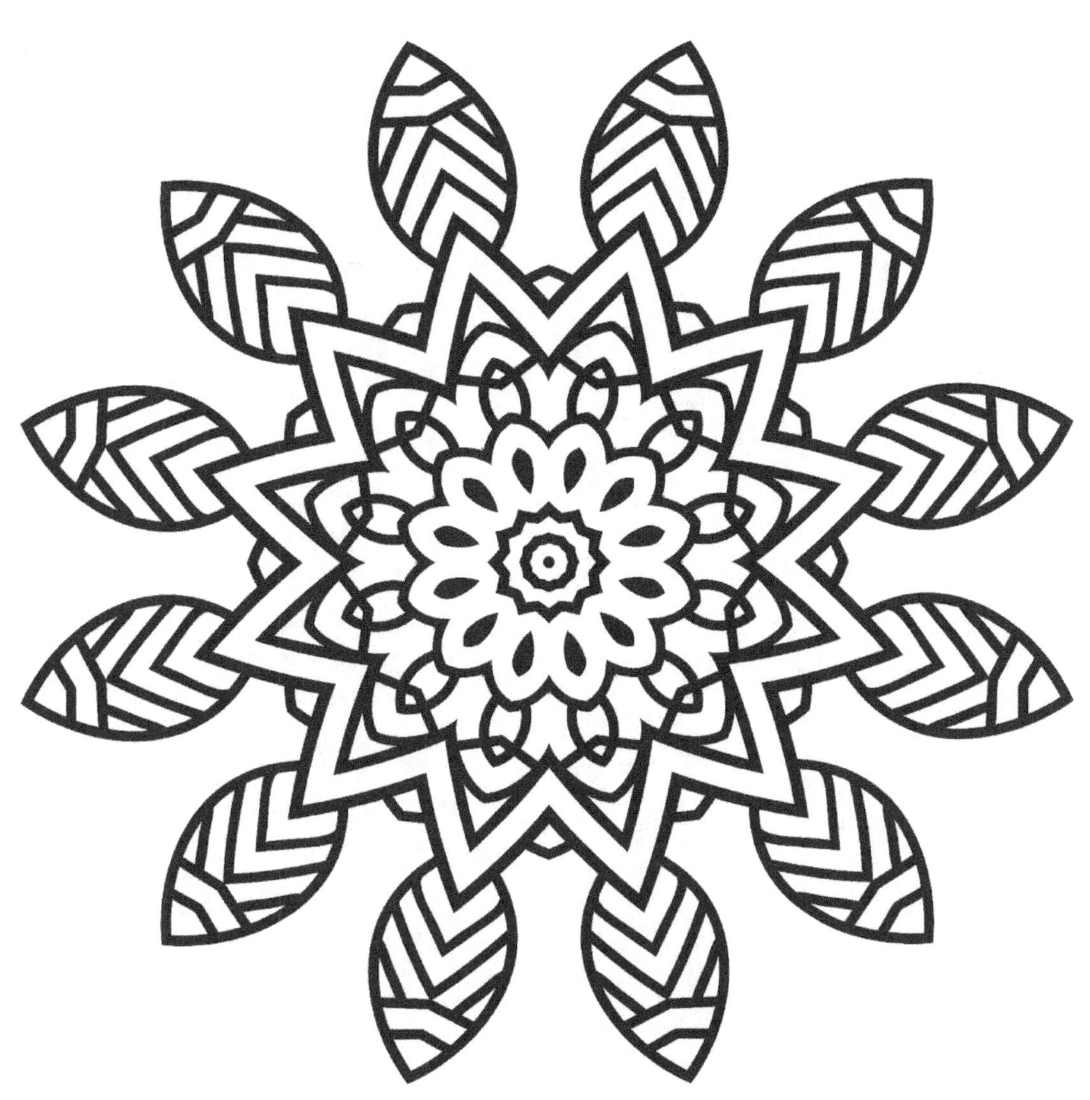

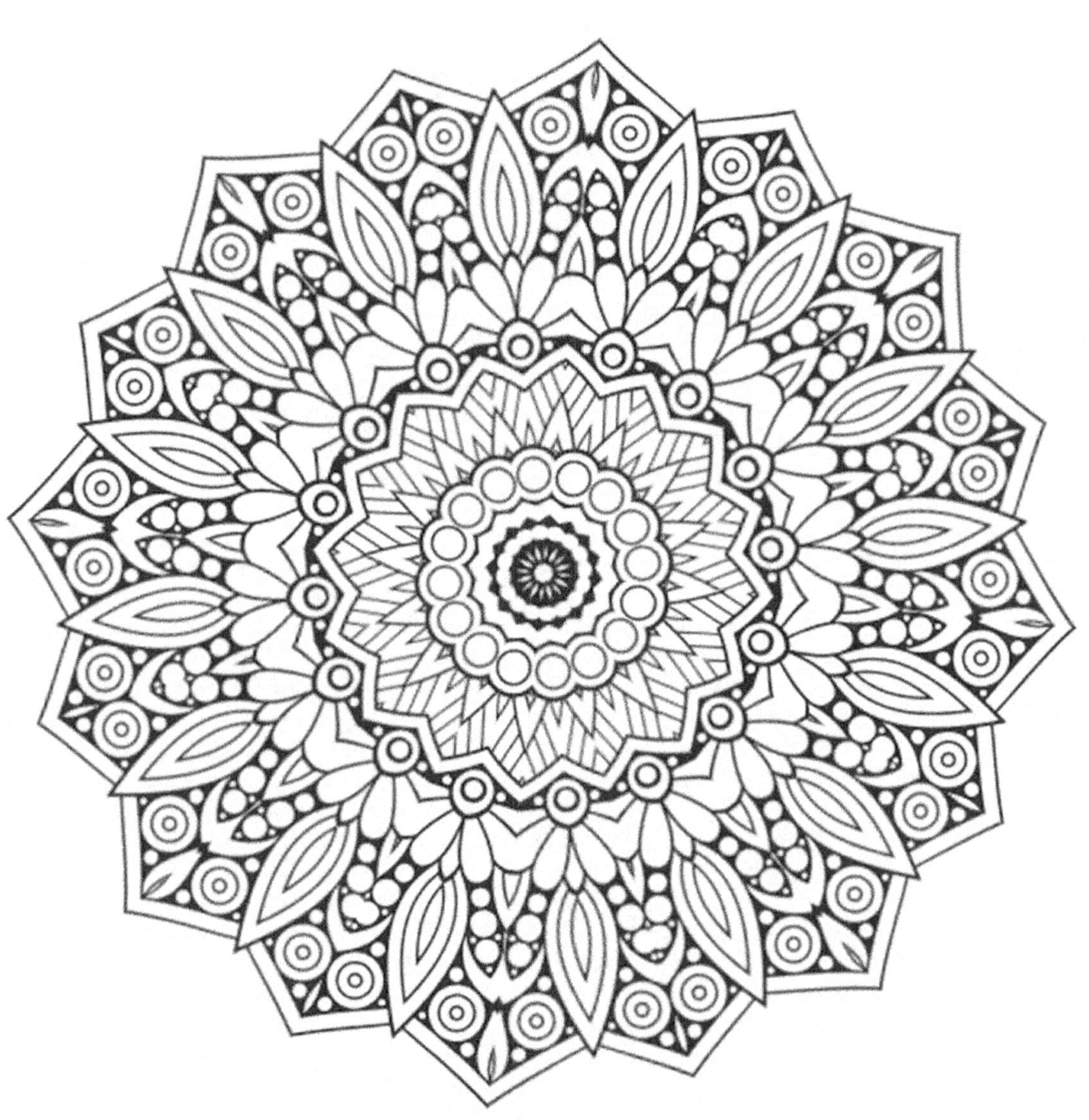

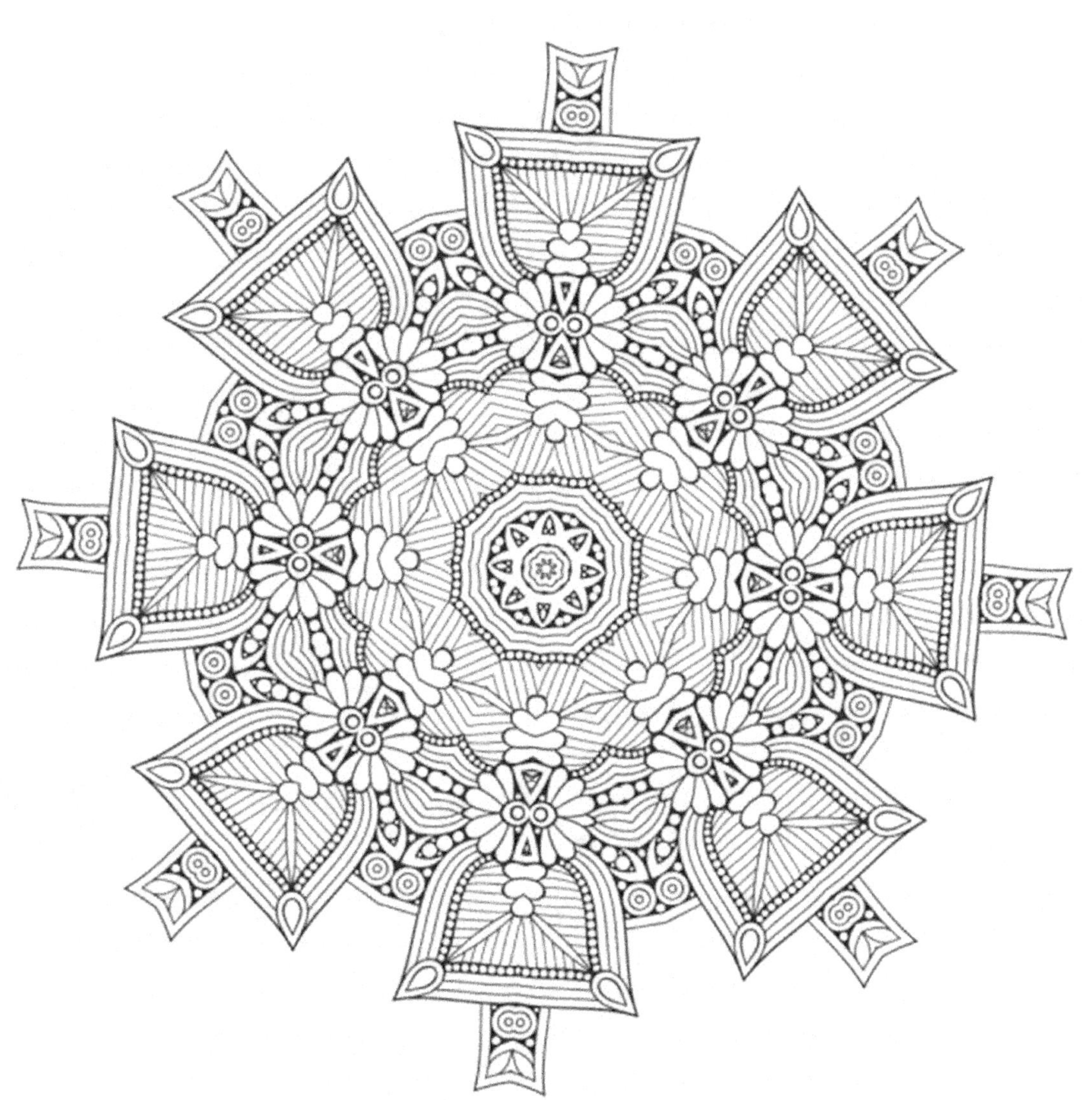

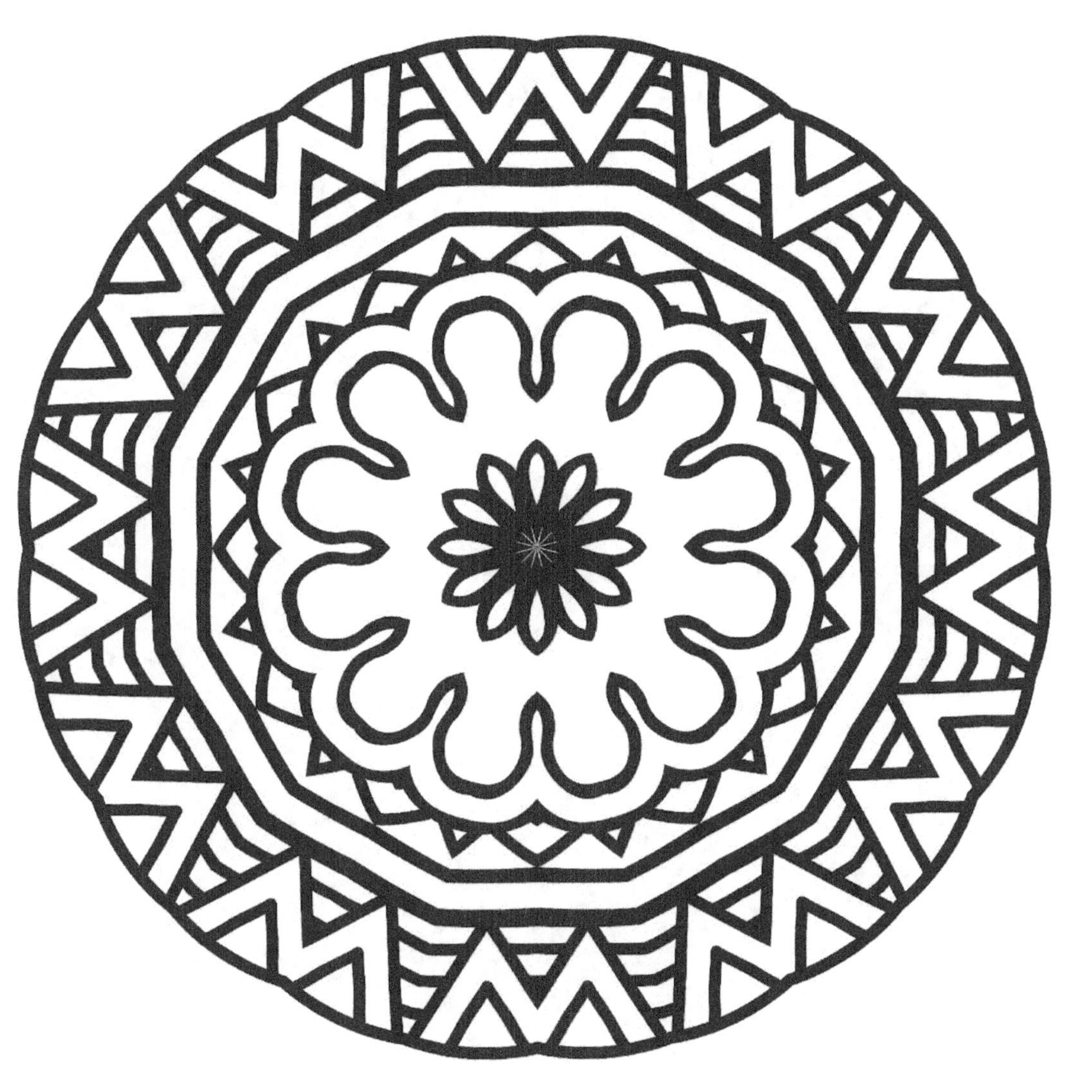

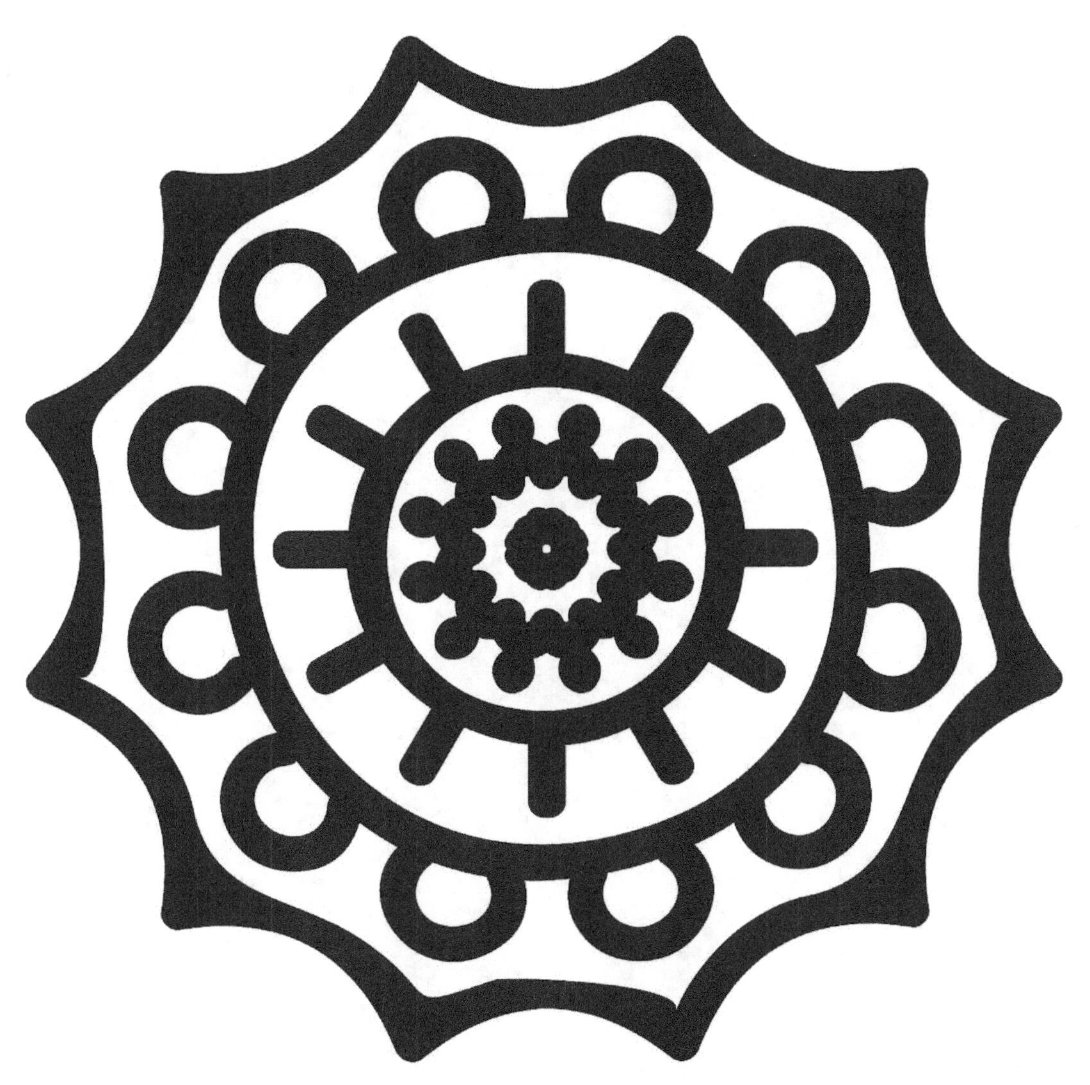

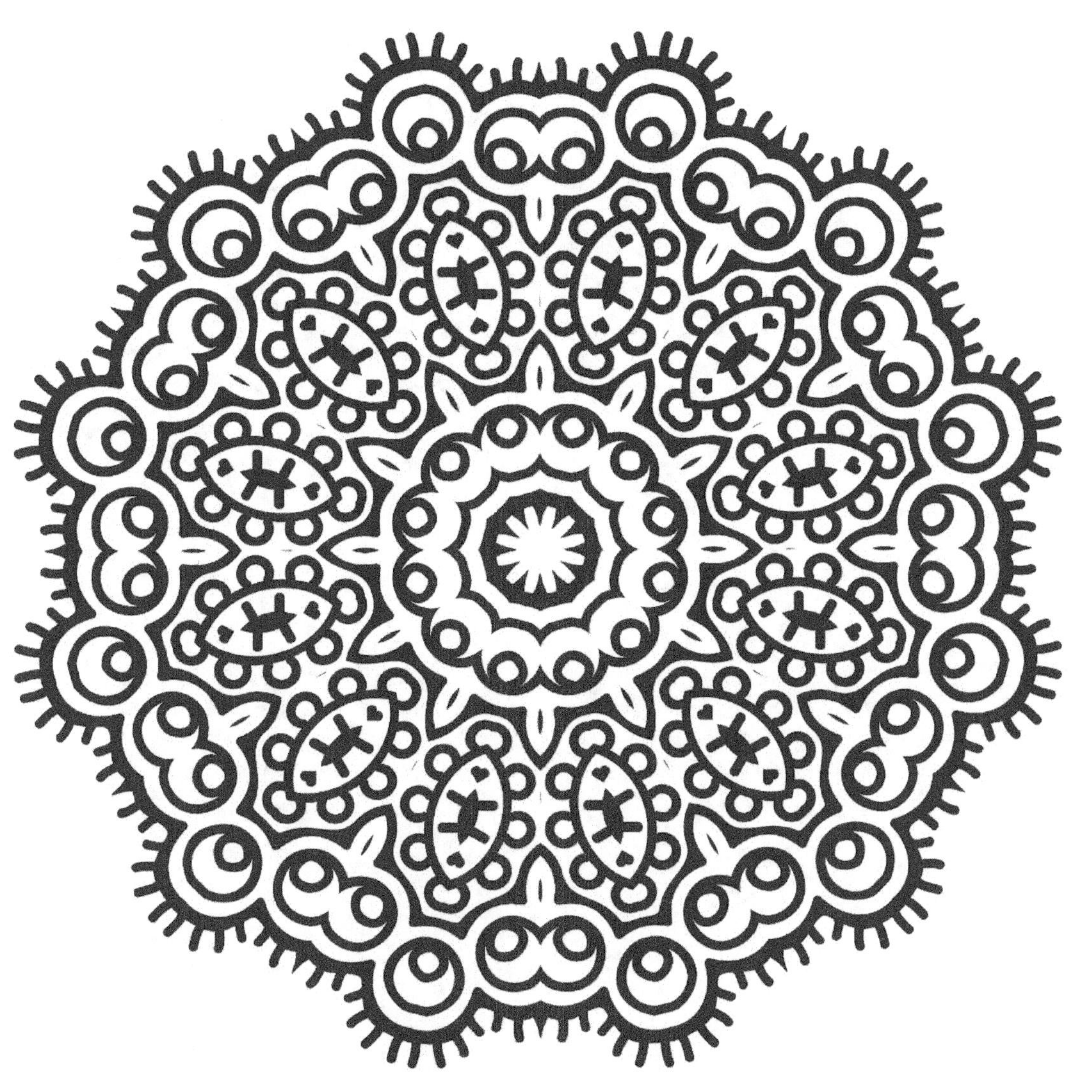

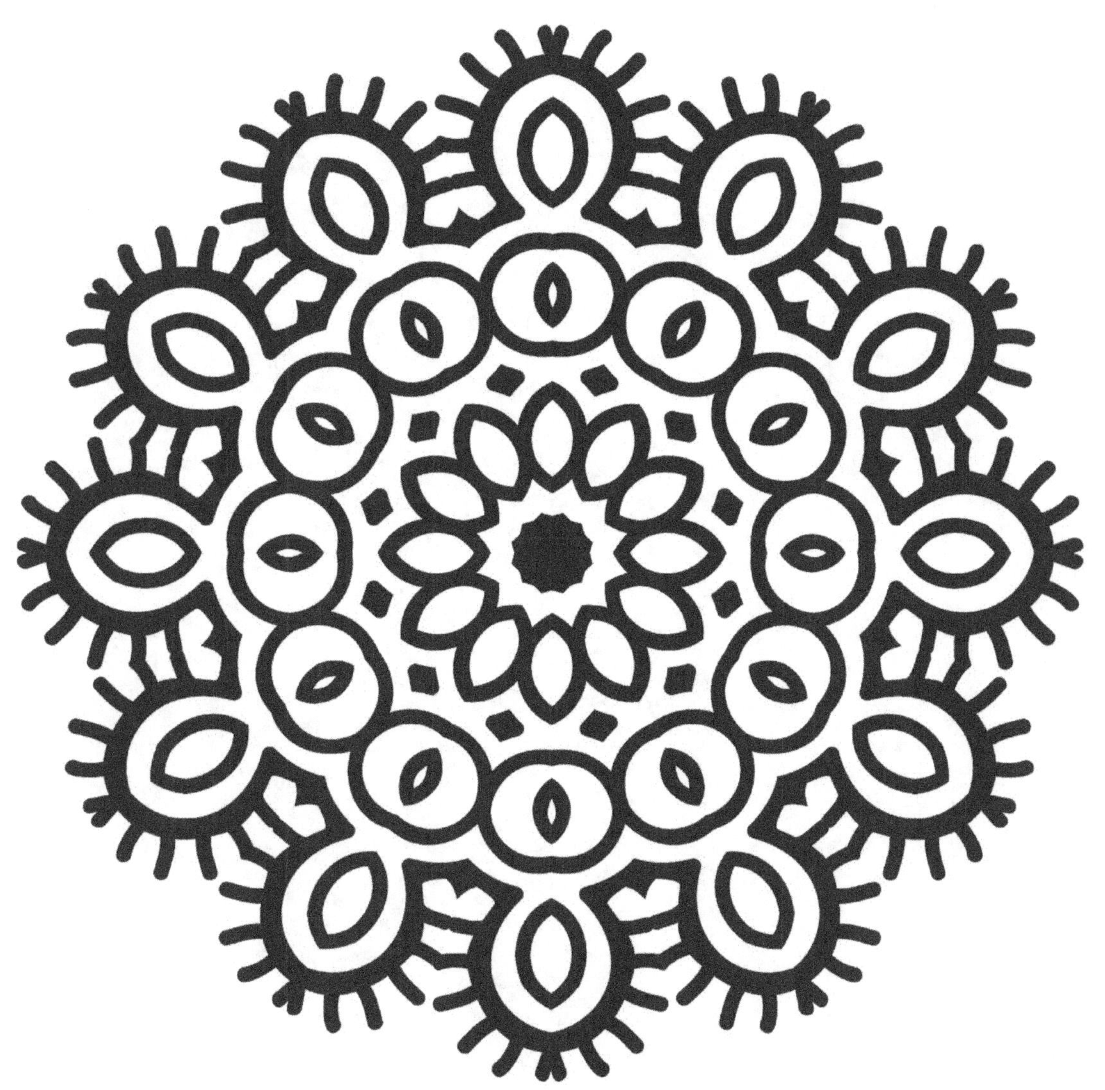

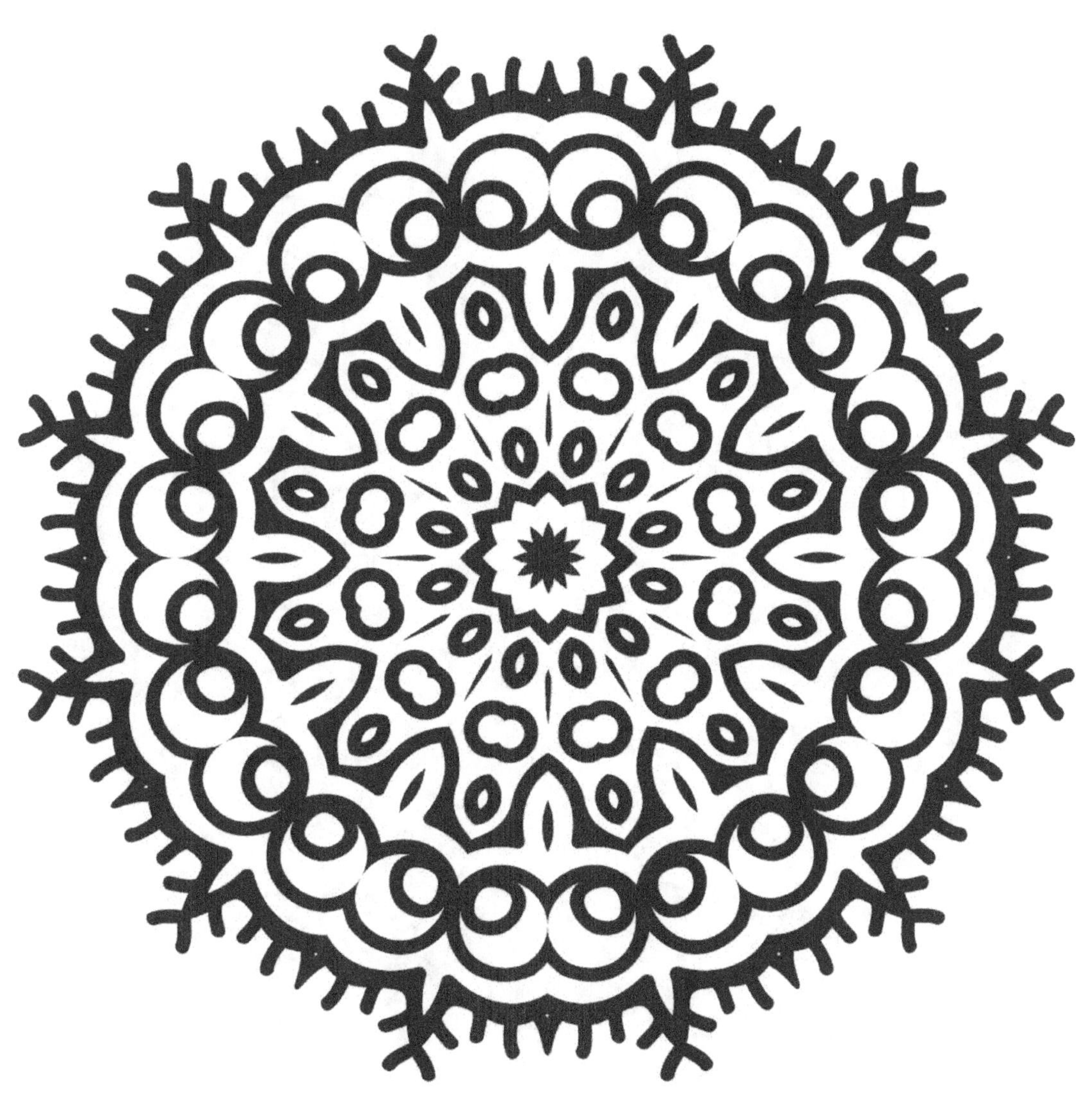

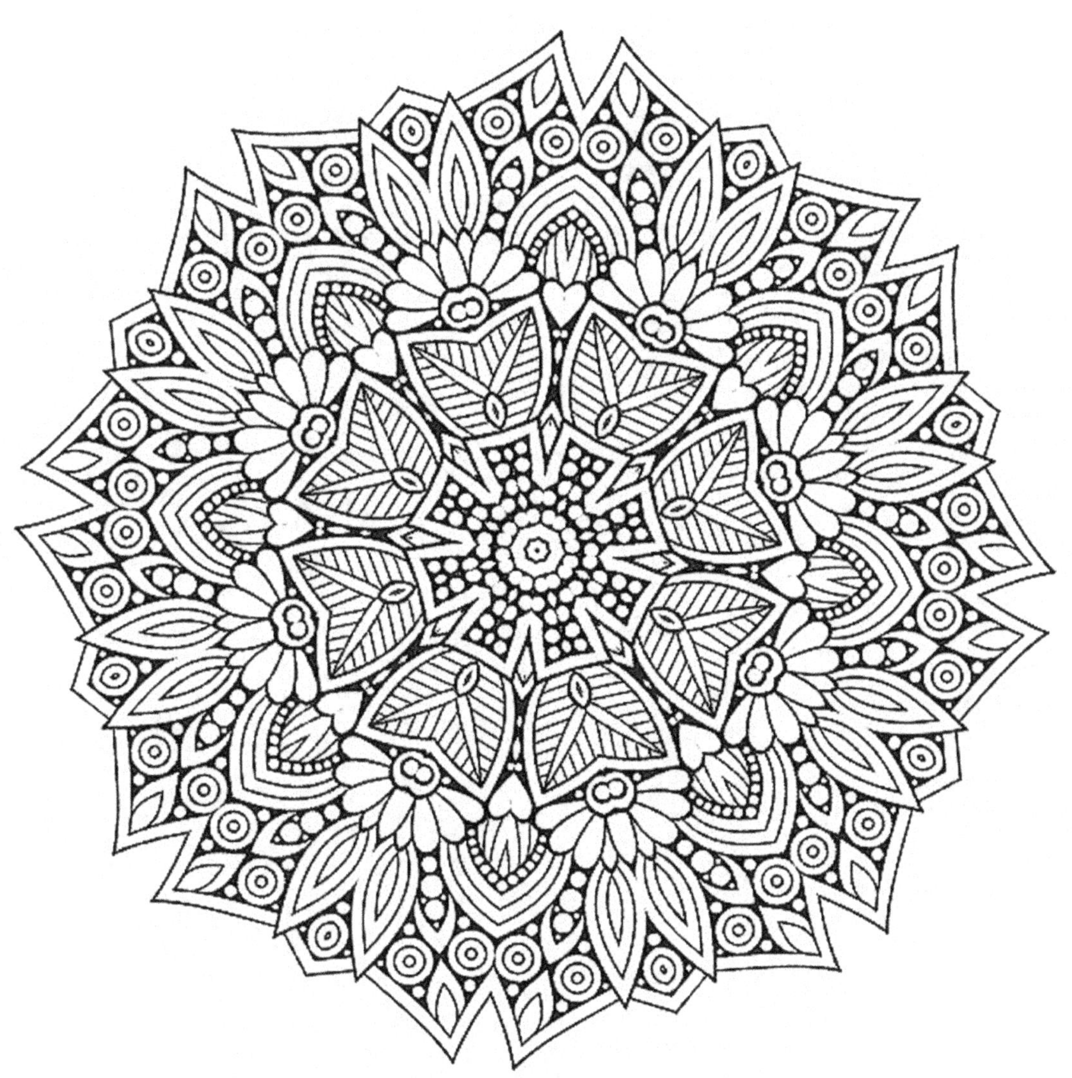

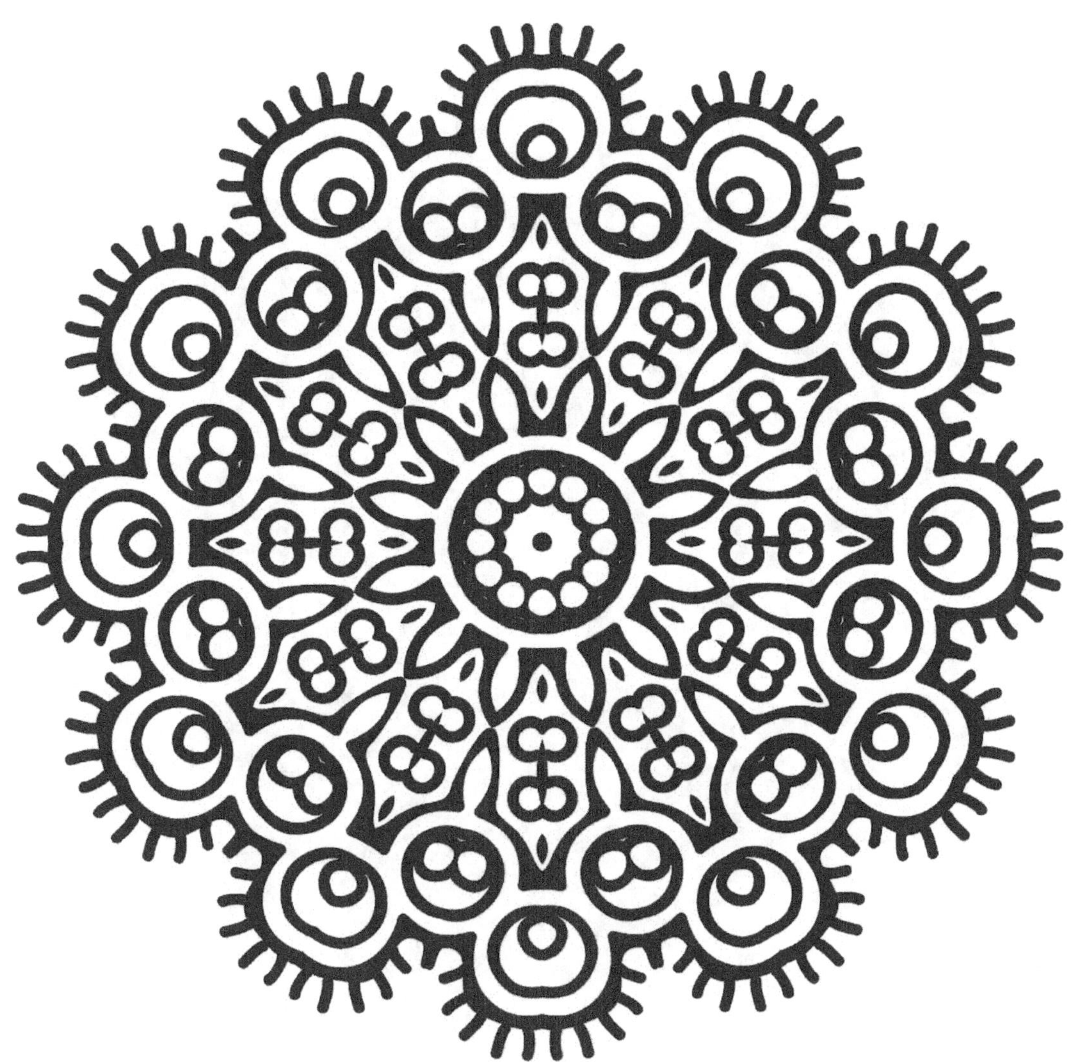

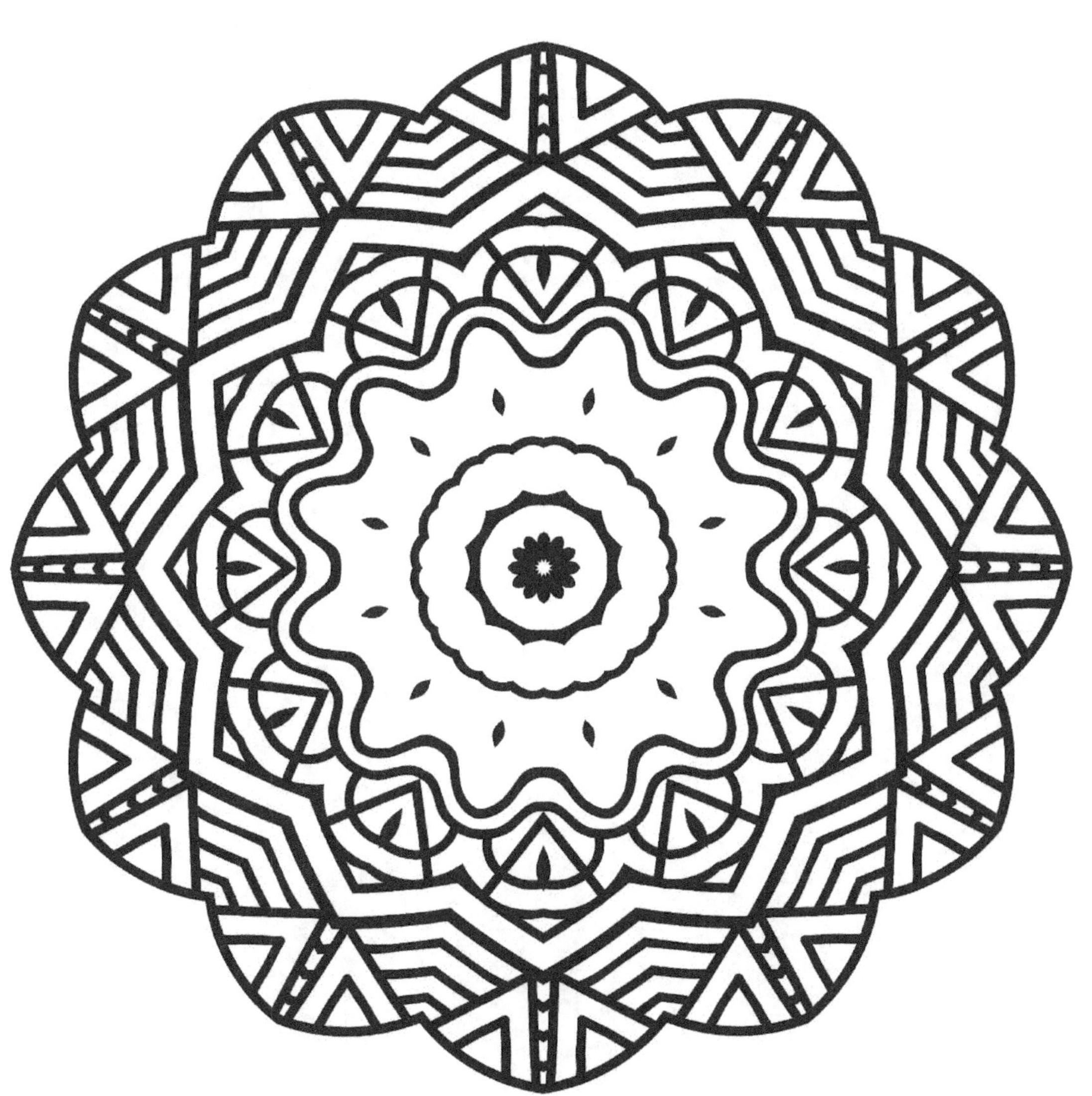

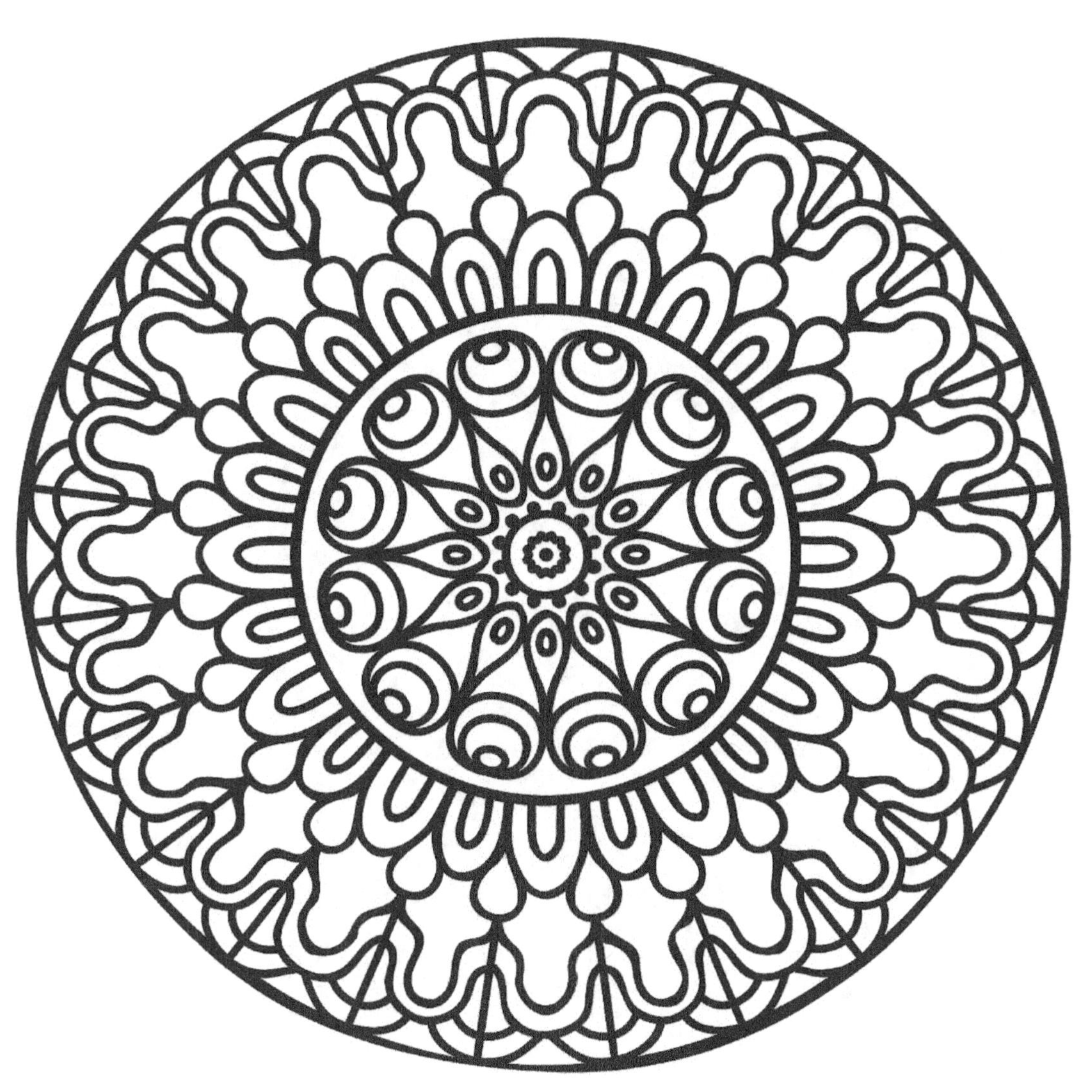

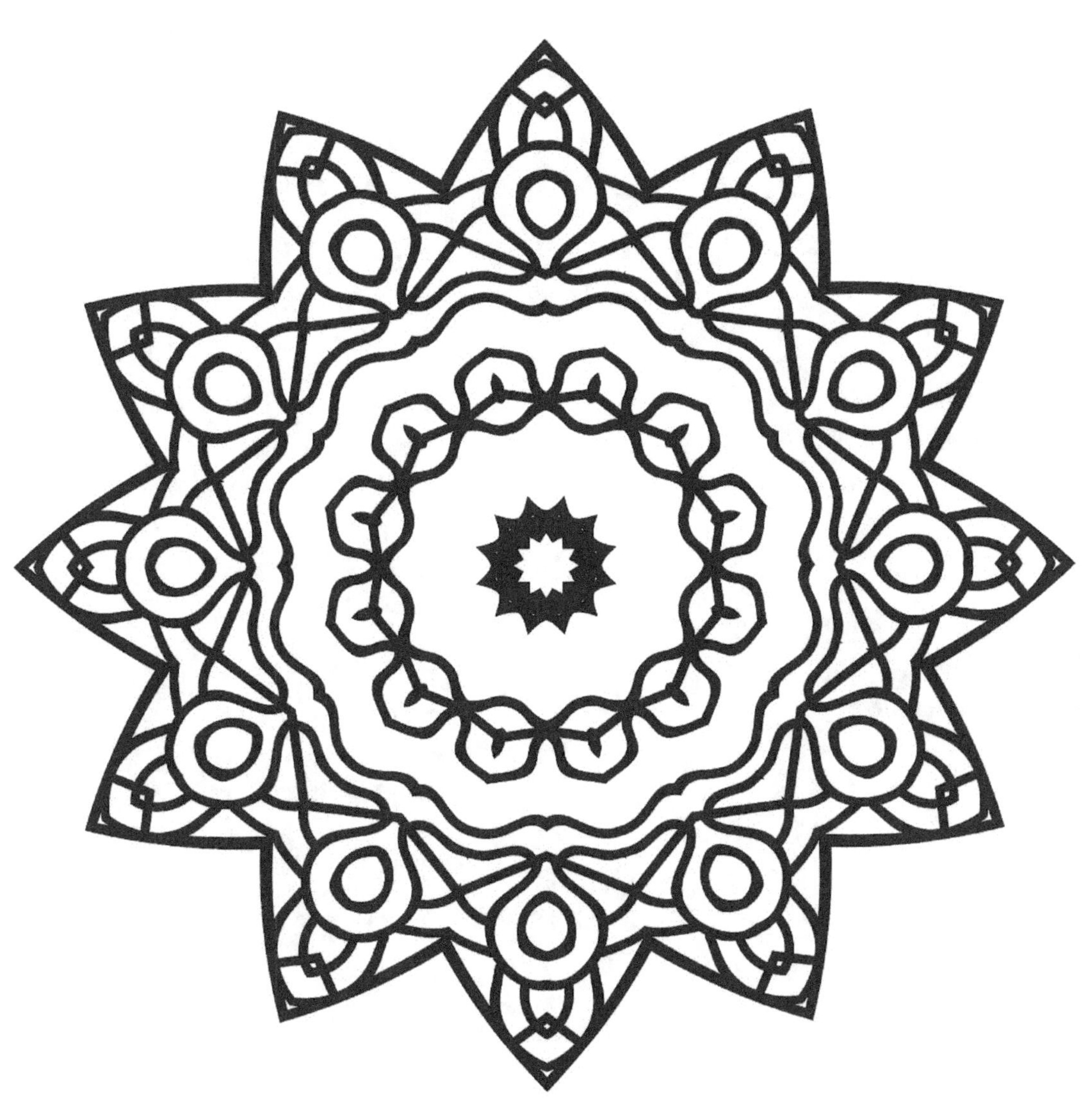

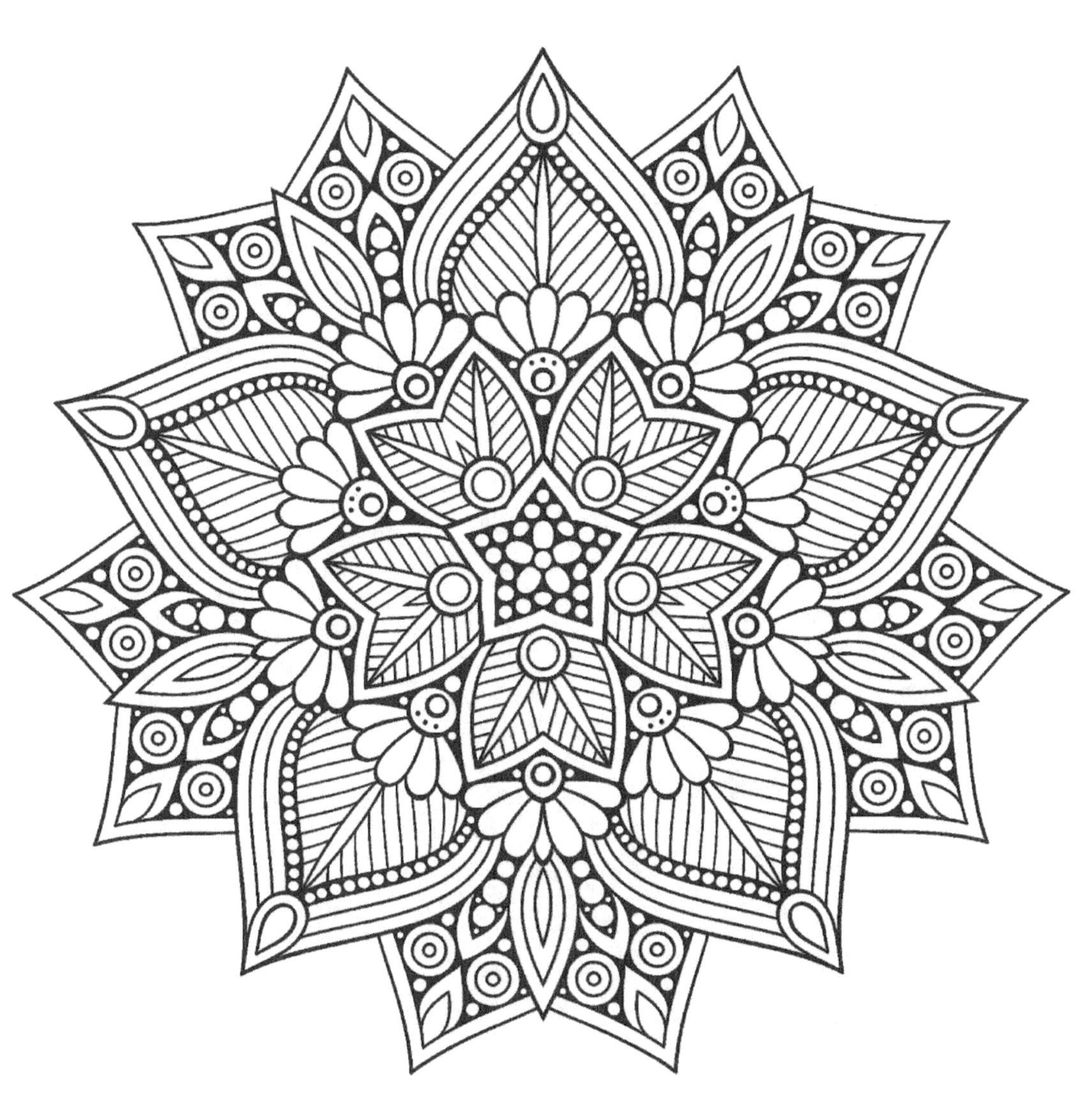

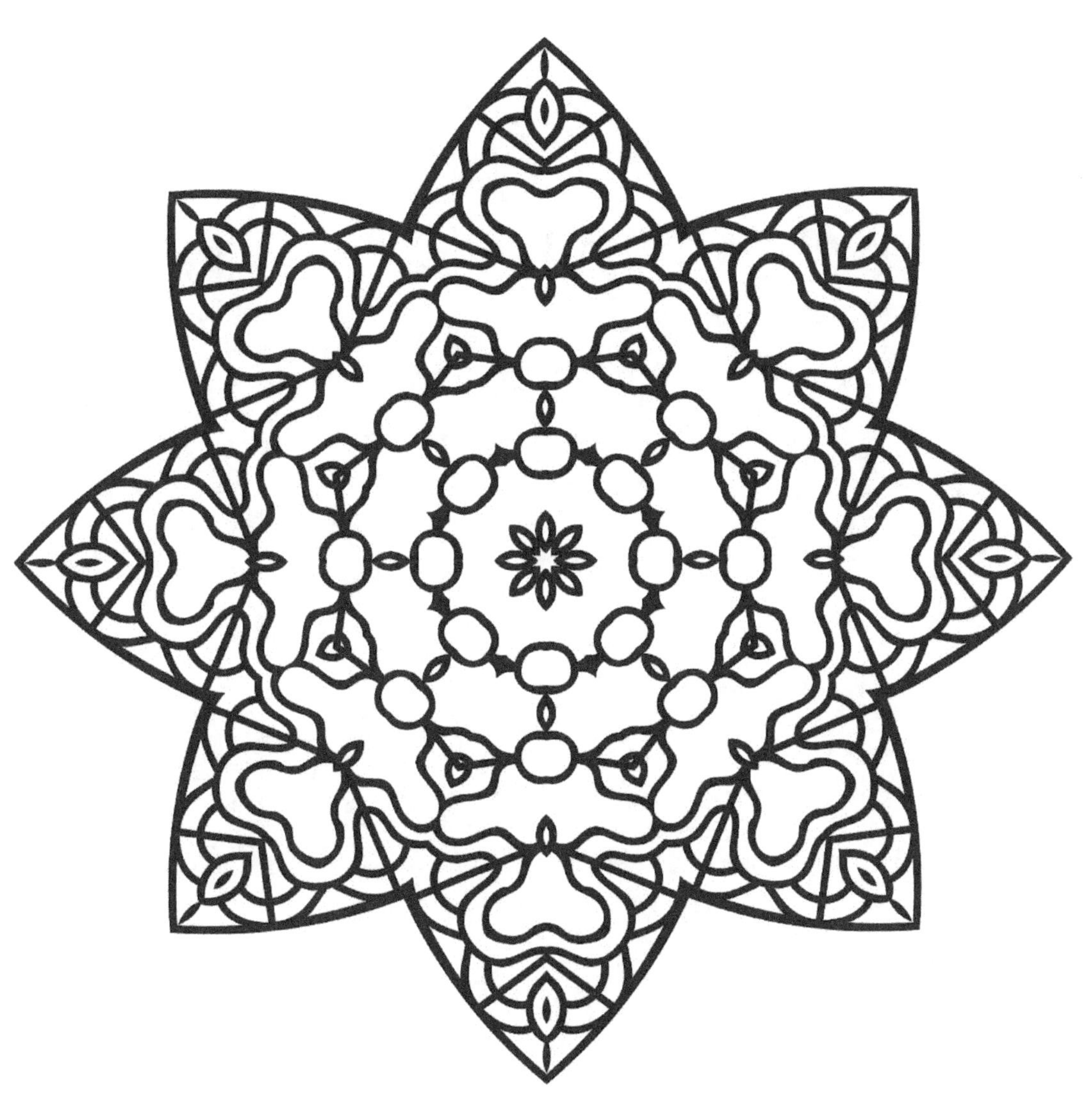

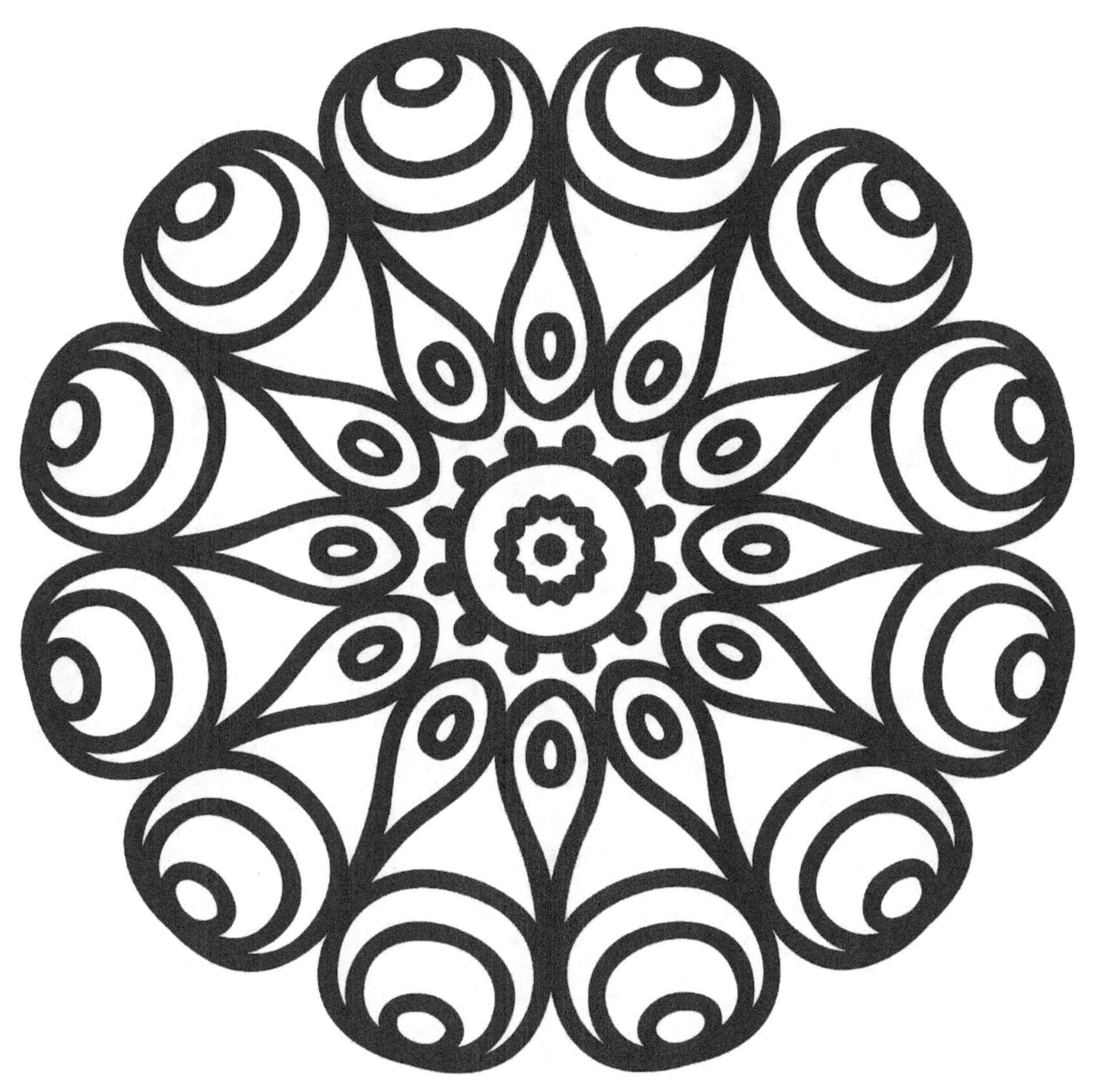

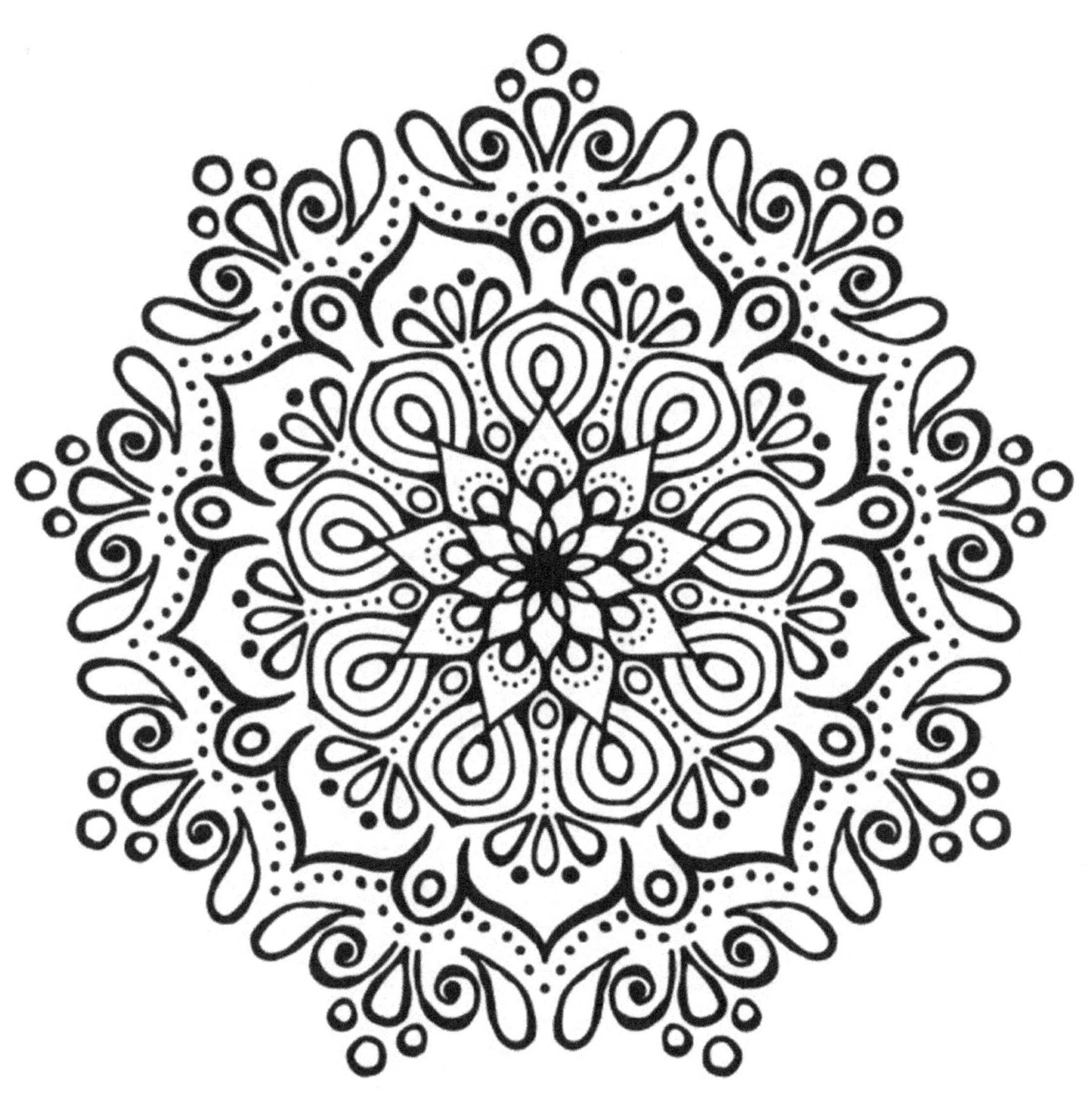